DATE DUE

GAYLORD		PRINTED IN U.S.A.

Some of these stories have appeared in *Rolling Stone*, the *Nation*, *Harper's*, *In These Times*, *YES!* magazine, the *Guardian*, the *Observer*, the *Los Angeles Times*, and on PBS *Now*, BBC television, *Democracy Now!*, the *Thom Hartmann Show*, and posted on *Truthout. org*, *SuicideGirls.com*, *Huffington Post*, and *Nation of Change*, and, with Ted Rall illustrations, in *Hustler* and the *Progressive*.

BILLIONAIRES &
BALLOT BANDITS

HOW TO STEAL AN ELECTION
IN 9 EASY STEPS

GREG PALAST
INVESTIGATES THE KOCH GANG,
KARL ROVE, AND THEIR BUCK-BUDDIES
WITH COMICS BY TED RALL
INTRODUCTION BY ROBERT F. KENNEDY, JR.

To our principal investigator, Ms. Badpenny. "I can see, Mr. Palast . . ."

Seven Stories Press
140 Watts Street
New York, NY 10013
www.sevenstories.com

College professors may order examination copies of Seven Stories Press titles for a free six-month trial period. To order, visit http://www.sevenstories.com/textbook or send a fax on school letterhead to (212) 226-1411.

Book design by Jon Gilbert

Library of Congress Cataloging-in-Publication Data

Palast, Greg.
  Billionaires & ballot bandits : how to steal an election in 9 easy steps / Greg Palast ; comic book by Ted Rall ; introduced by Robert F. Kennedy, Jr.
    p. cm.
  ISBN 978-1-60980-478-7 (pbk.)
 1. Campaign funds--Corrupt practices--United States. 2. Elections--Corrupt practices--United States. 3. Political action committees--Corrupt practices--United States. I. Rall, Ted. II. Title. III. Title: Billionaires and ballot bandits.
  JK1991.P34 2012
  324.7'80973--dc23

                        2012024742

Printed in the United States

9 8 7 6 5 4 3 2 1

"I want my fair share—and that's **ALL** of it."

—Charles Koch

"It is possible to exclude men from the right of voting,
but it is impossible to exclude them from the right of
rebelling against that exclusion."

—Tom Paine

Contents

Tales from the Crypt of Democracy
A Comic Book by Ted Rall
based on the Greg Palast investigation **135**

A Hostile Takeover of Our Country

by Robert F. Kennedy Jr.

American democracy is under assault.

In one super-PAC alone, Karl Rove and the Enron grifter Ed Gillespie, have assembled $200 million from big polluters and Wall Street moguls to buy the 2012 election.

Two of the Koch Brothers, Charles and David, pledged $130 million to elect candidates who favor unrestrained corporate profiteering.

The senators and congressmen they fund and elect are not representing the United States—they are representing Koch and its oil industry cronies, Big Pharma, and the Wall Street banksters currently mounting a hostile take-over of our government. The most corporate-friendly Supreme Court since the Gilded Age had declared in its notorious *Citizens United* decision that corporations are people and that money is speech. Those who have the most money now have the loudest voices in our democracy while poor Americans are mute. And the money is talking; in 97 percent of federal elections over the past two decades, the best-funded candidates were victorious.

America, the world's proud template for democracy and a robust middle class, is now listing toward oligarchy and corporate kleptocracy.

When I was a boy traveling in Latin America, I saw colonial societies that were essentially medieval police states ruled by outsiders in cahoots with a few wealthy local families. Those homegrown oligarchs controlled the land and the resources and traded the presidency among themselves. Maintaining such power required these cohorts to build propaganda machines to deceive the public, control the press, fix elections, break unions, and maintain a strong and often brutal police state in the name of "national security."

America today is looking more and more like a colonial economy, with a system increasingly tilted toward enriching the wealthy 1 percent and serving the mercantile needs of multinational corporations with little allegiance to our country. These radical forces already dominate the national press, with Fox News and talk radio snugly in the pocket of the corporate Right. This is the first time in American history that corporate and media interests have been so clearly and so perilously aligned.

With the media in their hands, and unlimited money, the final strategy of Rove, Koch, the Chamber of Commerce, and others of that ilk is to permanently cripple representative democracy by stopping Americans from voting. A boatload of new Jim Crow laws target Democrats by erecting impediments that deter poor and minority communities, senior citizens, and students from exercising their franchise.

Voter suppression is a crime. Nevertheless, sophisticated illegal voter suppression methodologies like "caging" are widely used by the national Republican Party to suppress minority votes. Voter "caging," for example, is illegal [see Chapter 15, "Karl Rove Confidential"] under the Voting Rights Act, and under a federal court order that specifically enjoins the Republican Party from engaging in this outlaw practice. Nevertheless, as Greg Palast has demonstrated, Republican officials, in defiance of that order, continue to practice illegal caging on a widespread basis. And today, this outlaw strategy is rarely prosecuted.

More worrisome are legislative capers designed by Rove and his cronies and passed by Republican legislatures across the country designed to purge voter rolls of Democratic voters or to erect onerous impediments for voting. According to the Brennan Center for Justice, there were no voter ID requirements prior to 2006. But since 2011, Republican strategists have introduced 141 voter restriction statutes in 41 states. Sixteen states have enacted voter suppression laws that will affect the election of 214 electors, 79 percent of the electoral college.

In 1778, our country was the only democracy on the globe. Now there are 166 democracies. We are the template. But while we are hemorrhaging blood and treasure to build democracies in Iraq and Afghanistan, our government and party officials are doing everything in their power to make it difficult for people to vote at home.

As Karl Rove recently wrote, if you can get rid of one-quarter of 1 percent of black voters in this country you can turn the election. There is something truly un-American about that.

At a projected $3 billion, the 2012 contest could be twice as costly as any election in American history. Billionaires are shoveling greenbacks into the campaign not because they are patriots, but because they want to dismantle everything that Americans believe in and love about our country, and all of the ideals that make us proud to be American.

Senator John McCain has called the Supreme Court decision in *Citizens United*, "arrogant, uninformed, naïve . . . the worst decision in the 21st century." The Court abolished one hundred years of American statutory law and jurisprudence that prohibited corporations from funding candidates.

These contributions are their down payment on our democracy, which they soon hope to own outright. Our campaign finance system has become legalized bribery. Corporate contributions grease the skids for politicians who mean to privatize the commons: to steal the air, the water, the wildlife, the fisheries, and the

Robert F. Kennedy Jr. reviewing confidential "voter caging" evidence during this investigation (Jackie Soohen for BBC-TV, RollingStone.com, and the Palast Investigative Fund).

public lands from the public for their private profit. Oil, coal, gas, and nuclear lobbies can now rig the rules that govern our energy policy to reward the dirtiest, filthiest, most poisonous, most addictive fuels from Hell rather than the cheap, clean, green, wholesome, abundant, and patriotic fuels from Heaven. Meanwhile, Wall Street is an unregulated and under-taxed casino where the public investors routinely lose their money in a rigged game that enriches the banksters.

For my part, I have no problem characterizing these corporate-centric super-PACs as treasonous. They are designed to subvert American democracy and turn our country over to the moneyed aristocracy. Their aspirations are apostasy to the notion of democratic governance that our Founders intended. We are now in a free fall toward old-fashioned oligarchy, that noxious thieving, tyrannical, oppressive species of government that America's original settlers fled Europe to escape.

In an article we wrote for *Rolling Stone*, Greg Palast and I first summarized the nine tricks of the new Jim Crow operation. In *Billionaires & Ballot Bandits*, Palast details each of these devious scams for disenfranchising vulnerable voters . . . but also, crucially, Palast here follows the money that powers the machinery of democracy's destruction. This is not a partisan issue. Clearly the GOP agenda is to suppress votes, as Karl Rove has repeatedly and unashamedly signaled. But *Billionaires & Ballot Bandits* exposes the vote-count blindness, biases, venality, and ballot gaming by Democrats as well. I don't believe there are Republican children or Democratic children. Every American citizen ought to have the right to vote and everybody ought to have the right to clean air and clean water, to integrity and transparency in the marketplace, and to a functioning democracy.

Greg Palast is the last of the great, old-fashioned muckraking investigative reporters. He's an "outlier," unafraid of corporate tyrants. Together, we have been investigating and exposing voter suppression for years.

Voter suppression is real. It's often a crime. And it's happening to YOU. But there is something that you can do to prevent it. That is the message of Palast's book.

Each of us has an obligation to inform voters that they have a right to vote, and that clever and highly paid villains are going to try to deprive them of that right. But we can protect our right to vote.

Start with page 285: "7 Easy Steps to Beat the Ballot Bandits."

Remember, this is YOUR democracy. You can do all the campaigning you want, but if your vote isn't counted, you're going to lose the presidency—and our democracy.

Read our book and download Greg's film, *Billionaires & Ballot Bandits*. Pass on the link, www.BallotBandits.org. And get the word out! There's still time to steal back your vote..

In the Beginning

In early 2010, Karl Rove met with a financier known as the Ice Man. The billionaire had more than his share of legal and political troubles, which would be solved only if the Ice Man could pick the next president and choose his own Congress. Rove said he could get that done, but it wouldn't be cheap.

The Ice Man said, "I'm in," and handed over a check for $20 million.

And he promised more, much more.

One way to win elections is to get the most votes. Rove has another way.

"Karl is the best political mind out there," says the Ice Man.

Way out there.

1.

Colonels in Mirrored Sunglasses

Here are the facts, ma'am:

In the 2008 election, no fewer than:

- 767,023 provisional ballots were cast and not counted;
- 1,451,116 ballots were "spoiled," not counted;
- 488,136 absentee ballots were mailed in, but not counted.

Add it up: *in the last presidential election, no fewer than 2,706,275 ballots were cast—and never counted.* I have not included a quarter million (251,936) provisional ballots counted only in part (that is, for some offices).

That's the official number I've calculated from the

records of the US Election Assistance Commission.[1] Approximately three million votes flushed away are ugly enough. But it gets worse.

In addition to the roughly three million ballots cast and not counted, no fewer than:

- **2,383,587 would-be voters had their registrations rejected;**
- **491,952 voters already registered were wrongly purged from the rolls; and**
- **320,000 properly registered voters were simply turned away from the polls when they tried to vote, mostly for not having IDs acceptable to a poll worker.**

Add it up again and the total grows to no fewer than 5,901,814 legitimate votes and voters tossed out of the count. Let's call it the Missing Six Million.

Karl Rove, when he was senior advisor to President George W. Bush, summed it up perfectly:

---

1   But, of course, the official numbers are bullshit. It's worse. How much worse, it almost doesn't matter: by any measure the noncount total is way more than the winning margin in two of the last three presidential races, and above the winning pluralities in a staggering number of races for other offices. For a detailed discussion of the calculations, go to www.BallotBandits.org. We are including, as well, comments and alternative calculations of the noncount by other credentialed experts. NB: The difference between these calculations is not large.

"We are beginning to look like we have elections like those run in countries where the guys in charge are, you know, colonels in mirrored sunglasses."

It sounds like Rove is complaining about Obama here, but I suspect Rove's really boasting about his own accomplishments under Mr. Bush.

For strategist Karl Rove, six million isn't enough. Through several front organizations and affiliates, Rove and his comrades have launched a campaign making brilliant use of the tactics originating from the Red Scare and the War on Terror. Now, instead of the communist lurking under your bed or the al-Qaeda sleeper cell next door, they've created a new monster to fear, to hunt, and to destroy: the Fraudulent Voter.

There aren't any, of course. Or, to be accurate, so few you can literally count them on your fingers—about six in any year, not six million—half a dozen jerks convicted of voting illegally. In the whole country. But in Rove's echo chamber of fear, in the Voter-Fraud Hysteria Factory, these six become so threatening and dangerous that they will be used to take away the vote from six *million*.

Tracking ballot-bending tricksters, figuring out how

they game US elections and snatch the choice away from the electorate, that's my job, my beat for more than a decade, for the *Guardian* and BBC television of London, and in 2008, for *Rolling Stone.*

I started covering the election games in November 2000 when I got my hands on two computer disks from the office of Secretary of State Katherine Harris of Florida. My team cracked the computer codes and found the names of ninety-one thousand criminals—felons—Harris listed to purge from voter rolls.

We went through Harris's list name by name. We didn't find felons. But most were guilty of VWB: Voting While Black.

"Purging" is one way to get rid of legal voters. There are eight more tricks, and I'll take you through each in turn. It was bad in 2000. It was worse in 2004 and 2008. But in 2012, it will be *much* worse. And in 2016, worse than in 2012.

2.

"Why Obama Is Likely to Lose in 2012"

"Why Obama Is Likely to Lose in 2012" is the title of a column Karl Rove wrote in the *Wall Street Journal* in June 2011.

It's not Rove's prediction: this is his *plan* to make sure Obama will lose. That's fine with me—if Rove prefers vanilla to chocolate, hey, it's a free country. But *how* Rove plans to take Obama down is contained in the subhead, and it gives me the chills:

> *"Even a small drop in the share of black voters would wipe out [Obama's] winning margin in North Carolina."*

Here, Rove is not talking about winning by convincing black voters to vote Republican. The key to victory is *pre-*

venting the black vote. Period. Rove suggests, with a wink and nudge, the Game Plan:

> *"If their [black voters'] share of the turnout drops just one point in North Carolina, Mr. Obama's 2008 winning margin there is wiped out two and a half times over."*

The smell of freshly laundered white sheets, brown shirts, and sulfur is unmistakable: The key to Republican victory, in the Carolinas and nationwide, then, is making sure black people don't turn out. Or, if they do, that they're turned away. Or, if they can't be turned away, that their votes are not counted.

If Rove can stand in the polling station doorway and block three million voters from entering and bulldoze another three million ballots into a landfill he can make the Ice Man's dreams come true.

I can report that Rove is well on his way to success, and he's only just begun.

How Rove and his compadres set out to do that—eliminate six million votes and voters—and how he and his partners have done it in the past to black voters, Hispanic voters, students, Jews, and any kind of Blue-ish voter— that's the story you'll get here. And not just Rove's sleight of hand, but deliberate ballot-burgling done by others in the GOP and—*cover the children's ears!*—Democrats too.

■ ■ ■

When voting-rights attorney Robert F. Kennedy Jr. joined our investigations team in 2008, he examined the latest documents we'd squirreled out of Republican Party headquarters' files. And then he said, speaking of Karl Rove and his associate Tim Griffin, "What they did was absolutely illegal—and they knew it *and they did it anyway*. Griffin should be in jail."

But Griffin's not in jail, he's in Congress. Rove is not in prison, either. According to IRS records, he's director of a nonprofit "social welfare" organization. American Crossroads GPS, tax-exempt under section 501(c)(4) of the tax code, aims to improve society's welfare by dragging Democrats out of their seats in Congress and removing The Black One from the White House.

Let me be clear: whether Obama is reelected, that's none of my business. As a journalist, I stay clear of cuddling up to candidates of either party. *Who* gets elected, well, that's *your* problem, gringo.

I'm a reporter, and it's not my job to preserve Democrats. But preserving *democracy*, with that fragile little *d*, that means something to me.

3

Lynching by Laptop

Paul Maez, a.k.a. Pecos Paul, found his name missing from the voter rolls of San Miguel, New Mexico. How did that happen? Pecos told me, "Don't know for certain, *and I'm the elections supervisor.*"

In one Chicano precinct in New Mexico, no one chose a president. Hundreds voted, *but every ballot was blank.*

In 2004 in New Mexico, there were a total of nineteen thousand blank and oddly ruined ballots. Here's the weird part: 89 percent, nine out of ten votes destroyed, were cast by Hispanics like Maez or African Americans or Native Americans. George Bush won the state by fewer than six thousand votes.

In response to the exposure of Katherine Harris's mass purge of innocent voters as "felons," George W. Bush, elected president by this purge-gone-wild, announced that he would "reform" the voting system. The result: the Help America Vote Act (HAVA), crafted by Bush's Senior Counselor Karl Rove. When Rove tells you he wants to "help" you vote, *look out.*

AS OF JANUARY 1, 2006, EACH OF THE 50 SECRETARIES OF STATE BECAME EMPOWERED TO REJECT THOSE VOTER REGISTRATIONS.

(Rove had help from the bill's chief sponsor, Congressman Bob Ney, and his friend, Jack Abramoff. Because they added a few goodies for Abramoff's clients into the law, Abramoff and Representative Ney were imprisoned. Rove is still at large.)

The "reform"? Help America Vote now *requires* every secretary of state to do a Katherine Harris: centralize and computerize voter lists, then "maintain" the list; that is, use the same suspect software algorithms to hunt down, purge, block, erase, and disappear "illegal" voters.

It doesn't matter that the number of "illegal" votes

cast in America is statistically nonexistent. "You're more likely to be struck by lightning than cast a vote illegally," expert Dr. Tova Wang told me. *Sixty times* more likely to be struck by lightning (I checked).

Since 2006, over 100,000 have been removed from the rolls—and that's just in Arizona—for voters' failure to prove their citizenship. The fact that *every one* of these Americans are citizens, well, hey. In 2012, the Hopi Tribal Council sued because they've been citizens of America before there was America, so not many have some kind of proof except ancient arrowheads. Can you guess the probability you get booted from polling stations in Arizona if you're Hispanic? If you said 500 percent higher than white folk, you win a hanging chad. (The winner is Chief US District Court Judge Roslyn Silver, who made that finding before reading the Constitution to Arizona officials. However, the "Brown-out" continues.)

In Colorado, another electoral swing state, the Republican secretary of state used new HAVA powers to wipe away *one in five* voters (19.4 percent) off the state's voter rolls, double Barack Obama's 2008 victory margin. Why? Don't know. Notably, the names were overwhelmingly Hispanic. For BBC, I flew to Colorado to find out, but the secretary of state locked me out of his office and refused our calls.

Back in Florida, Bobbie Moore had been removed from the 2008 voter rolls because she was convicted of a felony crime in the year *2014*. I've found hundreds of Criminals of the Future purged from Florida voter rolls. Interesting,

Ms. Bobbie Moore was matched with the felon "Robert Moore." Apparently, before she commits her crime, she will have a sex-change operation. Of course, the one thing she/he won't change: her race. Next to Moore's name(s) on the voter scrub list: *BLA*. Black, like the majority who wrongly lost their votes. Here's a typical detail from the Florida purge list we got our hands on:

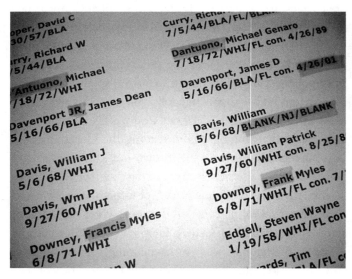

If you think things have improved since we outed Katherine Harris's tactics in 2000, think again: GOP officials ginned up this purge sheet long after Harris departed. The sheets that Florida and Georgia and Colorado are using in 2012 are more effective in purging the registrations of legal black voters than the sheets used by the Ku Klux Klan.

■ ■ ■

Only nineteen of one hundred Hispanics are registered in the USA. But not for lack of trying. Example: 42 percent of voters who registered in California, or thought they registered, had their forms rejected by the Republican Secretary of State [caps] and his Democratic successor Debra Bowen, who told us the Rejected Americans were mostly people with "unusual names"— Vietnamese, Hispanic, Filipino— that is, "unusual" for Republicans.

The chance you will be allowed to register to vote, to cast a vote, and to have that vote counted is directly proportional to the melanin in the skin of your ancestors. It took a Civil War to amend the US Constitution to ban restrictions on voting by race (the Fifteenth Amendment, ratified 1870). It took almost no time to overturn the results of the Civil War and virtually eliminate voters of color through a range of "voter integrity" measures designed by the

PURGING: Removing citizens from voter rolls, generally through computerized matches which identify legitimate voters as "felons" or "dead" or "doubly registered" or "legally insane." This violation of civil rights is usually committed by illegally insane secretaries of state.

Ku Klux Klan and the Democratic Party. Another Civil War, less bloody but not without martyrs, fought in the 1960s, again attempted to end America's apartheid voting system.

Now, in the twenty-first century, the Grand Wizards are back again to stand in the polling station doorways, to overturn the civil rights movement, but this time with spreadsheets, not white sheets. Voters are lynched by laptop.

In 2012, Karl Rove is building the largest database ever conceived, called DataTrust, under contract with the Republican National Committee, containing every US voter and potential voter.

To win an election, you need votes. Or, just as good, you need to take away the votes of your opponent. While winning votes costs money, so does getting votes to disappear. Purging and blocking voters on a grand scale—thousands and millions of registrations and ballots—isn't checkers. It's complex and very, very expensive.

Rove's Crossroads is collecting a quarter-billion dollars for its computerized Jim Crow machine.

Look, if Karl wants to pimp out his computers with profiling programs that would make the KGB envious, for the purpose of targeting voters for a spiel to win their votes, well, bless'm, that's democracy.

But given Rove's history (we'll get to those sordid stories shortly), you'd have to be a fool or a tool to believe that such data mining would not be applied to Rove's cause of saving America from fraudulent voters by identifying and challenging "suspect" ones. And the voters Rove most suspects are not too white nor too rich.

It's more than troubling that the first funder of the Rove-bot database and campaign operation was, within days of the *Citizens United* decision, billionaire Ken Langone. Langone knows all about databases. It was the database firm funded by Langone, ChoicePoint Inc., which crafted the faux "felon" list used by Katherine Harris to scrub innocent black voters in 2000.[2]

Now Big Brother Rove has some fierce, if friendly, competition from Bigger Brothers, Charles and David Koch, who have crafted a data-mining operation called Themis.

To make use of Themis, the Kochs are putting together their own quarter-billion-dollar operation, Americans for Prosperity.

The Democrats? They're still playing with their floppy disks.

The half-billion-dollar pokey put together by Rove and the Koch Oil Brothers is the down payment on a new uncivil, antirights movement. America's voting apartheid is now digitized. In all, we can expect over five million voters to be convicted of the crime of fraudulent voting

---

2   Langone had little financial interest in database management, but major financial interest in eliminating the rules against insider trading and stock market manipulation. New York State Attorney General Eliot Spitzer charged Langone with market manipulation in a civil action. It appears that Mr. Langone was behind obtaining information on Spitzer's late-night snacking. See "Eliot's Mess" at www.BallotBandits.org.

and sentenced to losing their right of enfranchisement in 2012 by the coordinated operations of private-funded and state-funded Jim Crow software. They're not guilty; the software is.

Technically, the super-PACs and "social welfare" organizations are independent of the candidates. Think of them as the unacknowledged armed wings of the campaigns. (And indeed, the candidates really don't control the PAC-men; the PAC-men control the candidates.)

In June 2012, the Democratic Party and desperate allies in organized labor got their clocks cleaned. Republican Wisconsin Governor Scott Walker, despite late polls showing a tight race, crushed his Democratic opponent in a special "recall" election. While Walker's campaign officially outspent the Democrat eight dollars to one, this was only the tip of the cash-berg. Those semi-billion-dollar babies, DataTrust and Themis, went for a test drive.

Weirdly, Wisconsin voter registrations show a drop of 107,000 in the first six months of 2011, even before a mass attack on the list by the GOP-controlled legislature. Despite the fact that Wisconsin has no known history of fictional or dead people actually voting, the cost to real, live voters is devastating. The "matching" rules that knocked out 42 percent of registrants in California are far more severe in Wisconsin; and in Wisconsin, first-time registrants must mail in ID (as must first-time voters). The result is that only a *third* of Hispanic citizens in Wisconsin are registered to vote. And students? Forget it: using a formula from the Brennan Center for Justice at New York University Law School, we can calculate that about 97,850 Wisconsin voters under the age of twenty-nine lost their rights due to the new ID law.

The difference between the last polls and the official count indicates several thousand ballots were ultimately challenged and rejected. Wisconsin state officials are withholding the exact numbers.

And Rove is crowing:

> *"In Florida and Iowa, Democratic registrations are down from their 2010 levels while Republican numbers are up. For example, nearly 29,000 Democrats have disappeared from the Iowa registration rolls since January 2011. . . . In Arizona, Democrats are down 58,000 . . . and there are now 176,000 fewer Democrats registered in Pennsylvania than in November 2010."*

Wisconsin in June is America in November. Wisconsin wasn't a "dry run" for the November race. It was a very wet, drown-the-kittens-in-the-tub test run.

The *Wall Street Journal* attributes the drop of two million black and Hispanic registrants to African-Americans' "disappointment" in Obama. They're so disappointed that, if the *Journal* is right, several million called their secretary of state and demanded their names be removed from the voter rolls.

Am I suggesting that Rove would use his database to challenge voters of color in Wisconsin, or anywhere? I don't read minds, nor can I predict into the future, but I do read "caging" files (see Chapter 15, "Karl Rove Confidential"), which I know Rove's op did use in Wisconsin in 2004.

4.

Ballots Inc.

In ancient times, before the Supreme Court's 2010 decision in *Citizens United*, the maximum amount you could give a candidate for president, legally, was two thousand dollars. And, until 2010, to legally donate to a candidate, you had to 1) have a first and last name, 2) be a citizen of the United States, and 3) breathe oxygen.

Then, in 2010, the US Supreme Court's *Citizens United v. Federal Election Commission* decision (followed by a lower-court decision, *SpeechNow.org v. FEC*) blew the doors off the limit on secret political campaign contributions. "Unnatural" persons—headless, heartless creatures called corporations—could now spend in election campaigns. And, unlike us mere mortals, these corporate creatures are not limited to two thousand dollars.

Less noted in the hubbub about corporate personhood was that the *Citizens* and *SpeechNow* decisions okayed donations without a face or name, along with political spending by foreigners. Charles Manson can't vote, but

Manson Inc., al-Qaeda LLC, and Putin & Co. can run negative campaign ads on the Fox network.

And maybe they have.

As soon as *Citizens* came down, billionaires pulled out their debit cards and went on a shopping spree.

What do these billionaires want? What do men who have everything want? Well, Congress, gift-wrapped, would be nice. The White House would be nicer.

Their first purchase after the 2010 *Citizens* ruling: the 112th Congress, elected that November. Normally, a congressional seat is a lifetime sentence, though a cushy one. Until 2010, with one exception in four decades, reelection rates in the House exceeded 90 percent. But, in 2010, incumbent Democrats were swept out on a diarrhetic tsunami of smear ads paid by new super-PACs, 527s, and tax-exempt social welfare organizations. Rove's American Crossroads did its part, spending $25.8 million mostly on advertisements savaging policy positions held by Democratic candidates for Congress.

There's an awful lot of loot paying for involuntary plastic surgery on the face of the body politic. You can look up the sums (at www.opensecrets.org) and (some) of the names. But what do they *want*?

In 2012, Paul "The Vulture" Singer, a billionaire, gave $1 million to Restore Our Future, a super-PAC. So did his buddies John Paulson (also a billionaire), Julian

Robertson (billionaire), Bill Koch (billionaire). Half a dozen other rich guys also ponied up millions to Restore Our Future. And a million bucks came from something called "F8 LLC." Records indicate that F8 has estimated annual revenue of only $87,000 a year. So that $1 million donation must have been a real sacrifice. The "principal" of F8 is listed as Mr. Diego Villasenor. No photo, so I looked up the F8 man in Google image search and found this:

Whether this is the *real* Mr. Villasenor, or if there *is* a real Don Diego, or if he's a Quechua Indian in Peru who believes photos will steal his soul, or if he has a soul at all, well, that just doesn't matter. What matters is the "LLC," which stands for Limited Liability Corporation. And under *Citizens*, the letters *LLC* mean F8 LLC can donate unlimited millions for political advertisements—and F8's owner's name, whether it really is Diego, his nationality, or even if he shot a man in Reno just to watch him die, *is none of your damn business.*

And what is Restore Our Future? Well, it is a kind of campaign Death Star that can and does emit crushing blasts of money to mutilate and destroy candidates who would oppose the electoral will of Paul "Vulture" Singer, F8, Bill Koch ($2 million donation), and the other billionaires.

In just the first couple months of 2012, Restore Our Future ran about $56 million through its cash colon to crap all over the opponents of Mitt Romney's presidential bid. (Official records showed 87.4 percent of the super-PAC's spending went into hate messages, i.e., negative ads and telephone calls.)

Buying a piece of the electoral process today costs tens, even hundreds, of millions of dollars. The Kochs were reduced to cooking for their friends to raise $70 million one night in Vail.

The Kochs' dinner guests were entertained by the comedy of Governor Chris Christie of New Jersey, who had the audience rolling with laughter (according to a secret tape recording) with jokes about cutting pensions and teacher posts.[3]

Christie then explained that gas and oil companies and the very billionaires before him were *victims* of a cruel government that stood in the way of the Lord and His anointed:

3 Hear the Kochs and Christie yourself on the tape obtained by Brad Friedman, in the film *Billionaires & Ballot Bandits.*

"All they do is layer regulation and taxes and bur-dens on all those people who just wanted opportuni-ties to use their God-given gifts and their ambition and their vision to try to improve their lives and through that, improve the lives of other people."

Amen. (But just for the record, it wasn't God who gave the Koch Brothers their gifts; they were Dad-given, inherited from Fred Koch, who made his fortune through oil deals with Joseph Stalin.)

Shortly after the Koch dinner, a secretly funded group called Committee for Our Children's Future ran a series of TV ads reminding America that Governor Christie has performed more miracles in New Jersey than Jesus did at that wedding. Remember that name: *Committee for Our Children's Future.*

The billionaires who picked up the million-a-plate tab for the Kochs' "Prosperity," and the million-a-pop kick-off for Singer's "Future," and Ice Man's twenty big ones for Rove understood this just buys them a seat at the table, just the first stack of chips.

But why play? What do they want? And as Butch said to Sundance, "Who *are* these guys?"

5.

Petroleum Porn: The XXXL Pipeline

Like all great American stories of wholesale plunder, the hunt for the connection between the unsourced hundreds of millions of dollars and missing ballots begins in Indian country. I was working an investigation of the theft of oil from the Osage Indian reservation in Oklahoma. This is two decades back. The Osage were dog-dirt poor, but they pulled in a couple of bucks, say thirty dollars a week per family, from the royalties they got from the oil under their trailers.

In the desert emptiness where the US cavalry had driven them long ago, greasy metal "rocking horses," stripper well-pumps, pull up a few barrels a day. Saudi Arabia it's not. It's not even worth running pipes. So the Osage contracted with the Koch Oil Company to take their liquid away in tanker trucks.

A tribal skeptic and troublemaker, the kind of troublemaker I like, Stanlee Ann Mattingly, would watch a truck suck out 240 barrels. And the driver would write down 232. Then the next week: 361 barrels out; 352 written down. Week after week. It's on film—taken by FBI agents hiding in the gullies behind the mesquite following Mattingly's complaint.

The G-man followed the Koch Oil trucks back to the loading docks where a tall, fit, blond man would exhort the drivers to increase their "overage"—the skim off the top—or else they could find another job.

The man, an agent told my crew, was named Charles Koch.

Way back then, I needed to explain to my *Guardian* readers that Charles Koch and his brother David, co-owners of Koch Oil, were the "richest men you've never heard of." And the Brothers Koch liked it that way. They operate America's largest private phone network outside the CIA, and they have no public shareholders, so reporting to the SEC is sparse and public shareholder meetings are none.

I'd been a racketeering and fraud investigator for twenty years already when I jumped into the investigation of the Kochs. Koch's motive for the skim was obvious: he wanted the money. But, for me, this was a new level of weird. Why in the world would Charles Koch, then worth about $2 billion, want to take *three dollars* from some poor Indian lady?

It even puzzled his own henchmen. Roger Williams asked Koch, who was literally giggling over the amount of "overage" he'd pocketed, why the billionaire bothered to filch pocket change from Osage families.

Williams was wired, and what he related on the tape has stuck with me a long time. According to Williams's recording, Koch answered:

"I want my fair share—and that's all of it."

But what *now*? Koch wants "all of it." Today, he has $20 billion and his brother David has another $20 billion. What in 2012 could a president give them that they don't already have?

To start with: the Keystone XL Pipeline.

The proposed XL Pipeline would bring thick, gunky tar-sands oil from Alberta, Canada, down across the entire US to Texas, crossing America's biggest aquifers. God forbid this beast ever burst. Some voters opposed this, mostly those who object to hastening a world where we puke out our polluted lungs into rising seas on an over-heating planet.

PT Barnum once said something like, "Nobody ever lost a dollar underestimating the intelligence of the American public." Nor, for that matter, lost a vote. The Oil-o-crat Party (Republicans plus oil-state Democrats) blamed high gasoline prices on President Obama, pointing in particular to his delay in authorizing the XL Pipeline. The XL Pipeline, said Governor Romney, would make America independent of foreign oil. (Governor, Canada is not a suburb of Seattle.)

Every Republican candidate announced that, even without a study, even without knowing the route or anything about the XL Pipeline at all, *they would immediately authorize it* if elected, even if the pipeline poured out into a church housing endangered species. Newt Gingrich has a magic calculator that somehow figured building the XL plus more US drilling would bring down the price of gasoline by over a dollar a gallon.

The attack is very effective with the public, despite its fact-free basis: Obama is President of the United States, not Saudi Arabia, the nation that sets the *international benchmark* price of oil through the OPEC cartel. I blame Obama for many things, but the price of gasoline and the laws of gravity are beyond his direct control.

Politicians' competitive lust for crude at all costs has grown from embarrassing to pornographic. Still, why all this enthusiasm for the XL Pipeline in particular? After all, there are plenty of other really stupid, dangerous, boneheaded energy schemes for Congress to blindly authorize.

Progressives looked in vain for the Koch Brothers' interest in the pipeline or in Canada's tar sands. But they were looking at the wrong end of the pipe. My question was, *Why the hell are we running an oil pipe two thousand miles to Texas? That's a bit like "coals to Newcastle," ain't it?*

The answer is: Flint Hills Refining of Corpus Christi, Texas—now owned by Koch Industries. In March 2012, the price to import light oil from Saudi Arabia was eighteen dollars a barrel higher than the heavy crude that Texas refineries import from Venezuela. East Coast refineries forced to import the premium Saudi oil were going broke, while Gulf Coast refineries like the Kochs' crank cash—so long as the heavy-crude supply flows.

But there's a problem over the Lone Star, and its name is Hugo Chavez.

Refineries don't just "crack" any old crude you dump into them. These filth machines are actually quite sensitive, requiring the right grade of gunk. In all, there are fifteen refineries in Texas designed to refine heavy-crude oil only.

But, since the fall of the American empire, the Texans no longer feel the love from Venezuela, nor its President Chavez. Chavez once told me he has extraordinary respect for America and, as proof, quoted Whitman at length. That wouldn't impress the oilmen in Texas who think "Whitman" is a kind of chocolate too cheap to buy for their mistresses. Clearly, there is a failure to communicate. Heavy-oil imports from Venezuela into Texas refineries are now getting scarcer and more expensive.

The Rev. Pat Robertson offered this subtle suggestion on his TV show: "Hugo Chavez thinks we're trying to assassinate him. I think that we really ought to go ahead and do it . . . This is a dangerous enemy to our South controlling a huge pool of oil."[4]

But failing that magic bullet, Koch's Texas Gulf Coast oil refineries will have to pipe the "heavy" in from Canada. And that requires the XL Pipeline.

With the election of 2012 approaching, President Obama could see the torches of angry citizens lighting the night sky around the White House. Angry white citizens demanded the XL Pipeline to bring them cheap gasoline. A crowd just as angry was made up of Green people who demanded Obama kill the great, black snake slithering down from Canada to Houston. (Well, that metaphor certainly got out of hand.)

So, Obama did the courageous thing—and announced he wouldn't make a decision on the XL Pipeline until after the election.

That assumes you'll be reelected, homey, thought the Brothers Koch.

The two brothers committed to raise a quarter billion to push the president out of the White House and off their Pipe. So they launched Americans for Prosperity. The *Kochs'* prosperity.

---

4   See *The Assassination of Hugo Chavez*, our film for LinkTV and *Democracy Now!*, based on the original stories for BBC television *Newsnight*, at http://www.gregpalast.com/store/?id=17.

6.

The Ice Man,
Radioactive

When the Ice Man told Karl Rove, "I'm in," he wasn't fooling around. The Ice Man, Texan Harold Simmons, is now the Number One donor to the Republican Party. The Ice Man, who got his nickname for his merciless, cold-hearted tactics as a corporate raider, says he expects to give $36 million to Republican candidates and nominees in 2012. Add in what he's giving Rove and it goes to well over $50 million for the year. Of course, that's peanuts for a man worth nearly $10 billion.

In the 2012 Republican primary, he gave $1.2 million to presidential candidate Rick Santorum to attack Mitt Romney. And he gave nearly a million dollars to Restore Our Future, the pro-Romney super-PAC, to buy ads to attack Newt Gingrich. He gave $1.1 million to Newt Gingrich to attack Santorum and Romney. He gave their opponent Rick Perry's super-PAC yet another million to let the governor of Texas make a jackass of himself on national TV.

What is the Ice Man up to, giving each one of these guys enough money to beat the hell out of the other? I can't claim to know everything in the Ice Man's head. He's playing multidimensional chess when I'm playing checkers. But, at the least, I know he's teaching all the candidates to heel, roll over, and beg.

He certainly didn't give a rat's ass about the candidates' positions on the hot-button issue of the primary, abortion and contraceptives. Simmons thinks all of them are nuts: he's pro-choice. It's not about philosophy, but, as Michael Corleone said in *The Godfather*, "It's strictly business."

Simmons is the King of Filth. I don't mean porn; I mean the stuff that can kill you, and does. His two big businesses today are NL Industries and Waste Control Specialists LLC. Their value, billions or busted, is completely dependent on government gimmes and rules: permits, environmental regulations, and the handling of poisons and taxes, of course—but most important, as we'll see, the law of torts.

His $50 million for Rove and Republicans is only one half of 1 percent of his wealth. As his candidates' tax and business proposals would easily boost his net worth by $2 billion, his return on investment could top 4,000 percent on just those two pieces of real estate called the White House and the Capitol. Not bad.

One investment, the $1.2 million Simmons put into Governor Rick Perry's campaign for president, is already paying off big time.

The key for Simmons was that Perry's run for president belly-flopped. The Ice Man is no fool: Simmons knew his fellow Texan was a putz and would crash and burn in the first presidential debates. So why blow $1.2 million on Perry?

Here's why: Texas law is, believe it or not, one of the toughest regarding donations to a sitting governor's campaign for reelection. But if that governor happens to be running for president, well, the sky's the limit. And if that governor ends up back in the statehouse in Texas, that governor knows who's pleasured his campaign treasury.

Perry's loony run for the White House, once finished, meant that Perry remains governor of Texas, exactly where the Ice Man needs him.

Why? The Ice Man's new big investment is Waste Control Specialists LLC. The Ice Man wants to take in all of America's toxins and poisons, creating a twenty-square-mile toxic dump in West Texas. But it was a dump without a hole. The business zoomed in value once the State of Texas gave Simmons a hole for his waste dump. The permit for the crapola was issued despite the unanimous objection by the state's own expert panel, which said the hole was way too close to the giant Ogallala aquifer, the very same water source that Obama tried to save by moving the XL Pipeline. It's the drinking water source for eight states.

Nevertheless, all three political hacks on the Texas Commission on Environmental Quality appointed by Perry overruled their experts and issued the Ice Man the license for his dump—not even allowing a public hearing.

In March 2012, after flunked-out presidential candidate Perry skulked back to the Texas governor's mansion, another one of his agencies approved Ice Man's superdump to take in nuclear waste, a decision made over the howling objections of Texas cities through which the hot junk would travel.

Now, toxic dumps have a habit of leaking and causing cancers. If this one leaks it will poison and irradiate the Ogallala.

And that leads to lawsuits. *No problemo, pardner!* Perry supported a voter referendum and lobbying campaign, backed by two million dollars from a group called Texans for Lawsuit Reform, which virtually eliminates the ability of Texans to sue for pain and suffering if they are dying of cancer from negligently leaked toxins. The two million for "Texans" came from the Ice Man.

For Ice Man Simmons, this is a two-fer—because Simmons's main source of billions is in the mental retardation business. That requires some explanation.

Simmons controls NL Industries, a name that beats the hell out of "National Lead," its old name, whose most well-known product was the popular Dutch Boy paint. The paint's brilliant colors were attributed to its special ingredient: lead.

The Ice Man took over the company in 1986 (Simmons virtually invented the hostile leveraged buyout). His stock quickly doubled, earning him roughly a half-billion-dollar capital gain. But more important, he was able to seize the company's treasury as a cash source for other raids. But there was a threat to the Ice Man's cash kitty in NL. The Dutch Boy was, it turns out, a mass murderer. According to the industry's own research, lead poisoning killed hundreds. Then it gets ugly: lead-based paint causes severe mental retardation in poor neighborhoods where the poison is peeling off the walls.

Example: In New York, Ana Amparo's son suffered "brain injuries, cognitive deficits, learning disabilities, reduction of intelligence, behavioral and attention disorders." When he was sixteen, forensic tests traced the problem back to lead paint whose chemical tags named the maker of the killer product: NL's Dutch Boy.

The key for Simmons to keep his billions out of the hands of NL's victims is "tort reform"—the political campaign to take away an injured person's right to sue.

Simmons appears to have bought himself protection from lawsuits by the victims of his enterprises in Texas, and he's made clear he wants to take his push for protection from his victims on the road to all fifty states.

When the lead-head isn't fighting retarded children, Simmons is fighting taxpayers. Simmons's company has refused to pay its share of the half billion dollars a year it costs to remove lead-contaminated paint from school-houses.

The regulations that removed lead from gasoline, paint, and most batteries have saved hundreds of lives and prevented thousands of cases of mental retardation. This makes Simmons crazy: he wants to eliminate *all* government environmental regulation—a philosophy you could call "Lucrative Libertarianism."

All candidates who receive Ice Man's easy-squeezy are pledging to eliminate the Environmental Protection Agency, but that's not good enough. In 2012, Rove's dogsbody, Congressman Tim Griffin, still not in prison, sponsored HR 4078, the Regulatory Freeze for Jobs Act, "to provide that no agency may take any significant regulatory action until the unemployment rate is equal to or less than 6.0 percent."

New York Congressman Jerry Nadler, sniffing the value of the bill to radioactivity king Simmons, formally moved to amend the proposed law's title to the Nuclear Death and Destruction Act of 2012.

But what's the use of a bill without a Congress to pass it, or a president to sign it?

As Simmons's ally, corporate superlobbyist Grover Norquist, put it, they just need a president "with enough working digits to handle a pen . . . to sign the legislation that has already been prepared."

Prepared by Grover and the Ice Man.

And that's what the $50 million in "donations" is for.

7.

The Vulture

A call came in from New York to my bosses at BBC Television Centre, London. It was from one of the knuckle-draggers on the payroll of billionaire Paul Singer, Number One funder for the Republican Party in New York, million-dollar donor to the Mitt Romney super-PAC, *and* top money-giver to the GOP Senate campaign fund. But better known to us as Singer the Vulture.

"We have a file on Greg Palast."

Well, of course they do.

And I have a file on *them*.

I had just returned from traveling up the Congo River for BBC and the *Guardian*. Singer's enforcer indicated that Mr. Singer would prefer BBC not run a story about him—especially not with film of his suffering prey: children, cholera victims.

Like any vulture, Singer feasts when victims die. Literally. For example, Singer made a pile buying asbestos company Owens Corning out of bankruptcy. The company had concealed from its workers they would get asbestosis from handling their product.

You don't want to die of asbestosis. Your lungs turn to mush and you drown inside yourself.

The asbestos company was forced to pay tens of thousands of its workers for their medical care and for their families after their deaths.

But then Singer used his political muscle to screw down the compensation promised to the workers. He offered them peanuts. And, dying, they took it. Like the Ice Man, Singer the Vulture used the cudgel of "tort reform" to beat the weakened workers into submission. With asbestos workers buried or bought-off cheap, Singer's asbestos death factories were now worth a fortune . . . and Singer made his first "killing."

Then it was on to Peru, where Singer had, through a brilliant financial-legal maneuver too questionable for others to attempt, grabbed control of the entire financial system of the country. When Peru's scamp of a president, Alberto Fujimori, decided it was a good idea to flee his country (ahead of his arrest on murder charges), Singer, Peru's lawyer Mark Cymrot of Baker & Hostetler told me, let Fujimori escape in return for the Murderer-in-Chief ordering Peru's treasury to pay Singer $58 million. Singer had seized Peru's "Air Force One" presidential jet; for the payoff, Singer handed him the keys to the getaway plane.

And by the way, I didn't give Singer the name "Vulture."

His own banker buddies did—with admiration in their voices.

What provoked the threatening call to BBC from Singer's tool was my film from the Congos (there are two nations in Africa called "Congo"). There is a cholera epidemic in West Africa due to lack of clean water. Our investigation learned that Singer paid about $10 million for some "debt" supposedly incurred by the Republic of Congo. To collect on his $10 million, Singer had begun seizing about $400 million in the poor nation's assets.[5]

Clean water for the Congo? Forget it—Singer and his vulture colleagues grabbed it all.

In Africa, I spoke with Winston Tubman, the former deputy secretary-general of the UN. He asked me to ask the Vulture and his cronies, "Do you know you are causing babies to die?"

It's legal, it's sick, it's Singer.

Well, not legal in most of the civilized world. Britain, Germany, Holland, and many others have outlawed Singer's repo-man seizures. In Europe, Singer is a financial outlaw. But in the USA, he's a "job creator."

Singer the Vulture gets loads of positive press, in the *New York Times* especially, where the corpse-chewer offered an open checkbook to any state Republican who

---

5   If it sounds complex, that's because today's pirates and predators don't make it easy to unravel their schemes. If you want the full story of Singer and crew, read *Vultures' Picnic* (www.VulturesPicnic.org).

would vote for the right of gays to marry. Don't think of this as an unselfish act of moral courage: it was more *droit du seigneur*, the right of the Lords of the Manor to deflower the virgins of choice on their lands. The Vulture's son wanted to marry another man, and so Vulture would buy the New York State Legislature to approve the nuptials. (That almost all Singer's money would go to national candidates who would make gay marriage illegal, well, money is thicker than blood.)

But, under press cover of funding the GOP for social rights, Singer's influence in the state legislature has paid back a hundredfold. He lobbied the legislature to change the law on the calculation of interest charges on his vulture loan-sharking operation, a change that will guarantee him hundreds of millions of dollars more from the Congo.

The Vulture's latest hit was a pay-off from the bankrupt government of Greece.

On April 4, 2012, seventy-seven-year-old Greek pharmacist Dimitris Christoulas wrote, "I find no other solution for a dignified end before I start sifting through garbage to feed myself." Christoulas then shot himself in the head. The government had cut his pension as part of an austerity plan to pay foreign creditors. One in four workers also lost their jobs.

Greece's creditor banks took their pound of flesh, but gave up some of theirs, canceling 80 percent of the loan principal. That is, all but two "bankers": billionaires Ken

Dart and Singer the Vulture told the European Central Bank and Greek government, *they wanted it all.* Singer and Dart would not cancel 80 percent or even 8 percent of the bonds they held, even though Singer and Dart, apparently, only paid a fraction of the face value for them only a few weeks before. Either the Greek government would pay Singer and Dart several times what the speculators invested, or Singer and Dart would undermine the entire bailout deal, bringing down the remnant of Greece's economy—and the rest of Europe with it.

Held hostage, the Greek government dipped into its emptying purse and paid Singer and Dart every penny they demanded. Singer's co-investors in his fund Elliott Management made a killing—including the "blind" trust of one Mittens Romney.

But the Vulture's gravy train of greed was about to run into an unexpected obstacle on the track. On April 4, just hours after Christoulas took his own life, in a courtroom in Washington, DC, the President of the United States and his Secretary of State hit Singer with a legal brick. Without any public announcement, without the usual press release and in language so abstruse only a lunatic journalist who went to the University of Chicago Law School would notice, Obama's Justice Department nailed the Vulture to the wall.

It was Ash Wednesday and Obama's boys drove those nails in: they demanded a US federal court to stop Singer from attacking Argentina.

In this case, Singer had sued to get millions, even billions, from the government of Argentina for old debt that President Ronald Reagan had already settled in a deal involving the biggest US banks. But Reagan's deal was not good enough for Singer and his hedge fund NML Capital. Singer demanded that a US court order Argentina to pay him *ten times* the amount he'd get under the Reagan deal. And to get his way, the Vulture also sued to stop the Big Banks from getting their own payments from the Reagan deal.

But then a bolt of legal lightning cooked the Vulture's goose: Obama's Justice Department and Hillary Clinton's State Department together filed an *amicus curiae*, a "friend of the court" brief in the case of *NML Capital et al. v. Republic of Argentina*. It wasn't all that friendly. Obama, a constitutional law professor, suddenly remembered that the president has the power, unique to the Constitution of the USA, to kick the Vulture's ass up and down the continent, then do it again.

Specifically, Obama and Clinton demanded the court throw out Singer's attempt to bankrupt Argentina (because that is what Singer's demand would have done).

This was Singer's nightmare: that the President of the United States would invoke his extraordinary constitutional authority under the Separation of Powers clause to block the Vulture and his hedge-fund buddies from making superprofits over the dead bodies of desperate nations.

The stakes in the legal-financial-political war are enormous, yet the real battle is hidden from the public view.

A titanic struggle had now been set in motion, a battle over billions, between the Obama administration and the wealthiest men in America, the hedge-fund billionaires, all out of sight of the public and press.

Argentina's consul called me from DC, stunned by the Clinton move. WTF? Did I have any info?

I said, this action goes way, way beyond Argentina. Obama and Clinton told the court that the Vulture was undermining the safety of the entire world financial system, destabilizing every financial rescue mission from South America to Greece to the Congo. (What would Romney do? His expected replacement for Clinton would be his chief foreign policy advisor Dan Senor—currently on the payroll of . . . Paul Singer.)

Does Obama have the stones to stick with his decision? And do Singer and friends, working with Karl Rove, have the money-knife which could cut them off?

The Rove-bots are already flashing their blade: in June 2012, Republicans on the House Committee on Financial Services held an unprecedented emergency hearing about the president's stealth move on the Vulture. They sat for testimony by Ted Olsen, George Bush's former solicitor general, who attacked Obama and Clinton with code words and inscrutable legalismo, not once mentioning Singer or his hedge fund by name.

But in the White House and on the top floors of the Wall Street towers, they knew *exactly* what this was all about. And in the golf carts on Martha's Vineyard, they knew the Vulture had to be put in his place. Robert Wolf, golfing with President Obama on the Cape, was furious. The CEO of UBS (a.k.a. United Bank of Switzerland), had put together the Argentina deal. And Swiss bankers don't allow anyone to move the hole on their green.

Wolf bundled plenty of campaign loot for Obama, who made Wolf his "economic recovery" advisor. UBS has recovered nicely (with a sweet plea-bargain deal on criminal tax-evasion charges).

Now, UBS, JPMorgan, and Citibank chieftains are lined up with Obama and Clinton. The Establishment banks look upon the nouvelle vultures like Singer as economic berserkers, terrorists in a helicopter ready to pull the pin on the grenade. If Singer's demands aren't met, he'll blow up the planet's finance system. In this war of titans, Obama and Clinton are merely foot soldiers, not the generals. It's billionaire banking-powers versus billionaire hedge-fund speculators. One is greedy and scary and the other is greedy and plain dangerous. Take your pick.

Here is the real battle of 2012—a winner-take-all war over the control of the world financial system.

8.

Penny's from Heaven?

Why are Barack Obama and Hillary Clinton so keen to take on the Vulture and provoke the wrath of his coven of billionaires and their mighty checkbooks?

If you want me to be a partisan water boy for the Democratic Party, skip this.

Barack Obama means "The Blessed One We've Been Waiting For." But *who* was waiting for him?

We never heard of this guy until 2004. Less than three years before taking the Oval Office, he was in the Illinois State Senate, a swamp of scammers, backhanders, and Party Machine tools, not a stellar launchpad for the presidency.

And then, one day, the Blessed One was visited by his fairy godmother. Her name is Penny Pritzker.

Penny's net worth is listed in *Forbes* as $1.8 billion, which is one hell of a heavy magic wand in the world of politics. Her wand would have been heavier, and her net worth higher, except that in the 1990s the federal government fined her $400 million for the predatory, deceitful, racist tactics and practices of the bank she owned on the South Side of Chicago.[6]

Penny did not like that. No, not one bit.

What she needed was someone to give her Hope and Change. She Hoped someone would Change the banking laws to let her get away with this crap.

Pritzker introduced the neophyte state senator to the Ladies Who Lunch (that's really what they call themselves) on Chicago's Gold Coast. Obama got lunch, gold, and better—an introduction to Robert Rubin, former Secretary of the Treasury, former Chairman of both Goldman Sachs and Citibank. Even atheists recognized Rubin as the Supreme Deity of Wall Street.

Rubin opened the doors to finance industry vaults for Obama. Extraordinarily, Democrat Obama raised three times as much from banking and finance as his Republican opponent in 2008.

So what did Rubin get for showering the Blessed One with gold? Obama agreed to take care of Rubin's poodles, Larry Summers and Tim Geithner. They became Obama's first cabinet picks, Summers as economics czar and Geithner as his czarina, Secretary of the Treasury.

---

6   Read the investigative report on banking à la Penny Pritzker by *Flashpoints* host and investigative reporter Dennis Bernstein at www.BallotBandits.com.

These were the two gents who, under Treasury Secretary Rubin, had deregulated and decriminalized the kind of banking activity that had got Penny in so much hot water.[7] Despite their banking-law destruction spree having brought the planet to its financial knees, Summers and Geithner were now back in the saddle—Obama's horse but Rubin's saddle.

Rubin received over $100 million from Citigroup (the commercial bank–investment bank–casino created by deregulation). His payoff went unchallenged by Citi's new owner, the US Treasury, which put up over a *trillion* dollars in loans and guarantees to pull Rubin's creature out of bankruptcy.

But now the centi-millionaires like Rubin are worried. Obama, once elected, protected the banks from doom and public anger—but not from the threat of the hedge-fund billionaires like Singer the Vulture, who has sued Citibank along with the treasury of Argentina. Romney's vultures have targeted the Congo, Greece, *and* the big New York banks that need to keep these nations alive.

The trillion-dollar high-stakes showdown between these finance superpowers, the billionaires versus the bankers, will be played out in 2012 and beyond, with

---

7   Our team obtained a confidential memo from Geithner to Summers, "As we enter the endgame," revealing the secret meetings with Citibank, a genesis document of the current worldwide financial disaster, which can be seen at www.VulturesPicnic.org in the File Cabinet.

super-PACs, supercomputers, voter-roll purges, senators, congressmen, and the White House as the pieces on the chessboard moved by the invisible hands.

But Penny is pissed off. She had taken a state senator/community organizer from the ghetto, made him a US senator, then, as the Obama campaign finance director, raised a mind-blowing three quarters of a billion dollars to make him president. In return, Obama decided to make his *patron* the secretary of commerce.

But then, just as he was about to submit her nomination to Congress, a bunch of Penny's victims marched on Washington. They were not from her busted bank but unhappy workers from the lucrative nursing homes which her family owns through a string of complex offshore trusts. Obama dumped Penny pronto.

In 2012, Obama, to his credit, snapped the door shut on Penny, reducing her to hosting an Obama reelection fundraiser at her Gold Coast digs, which she had to bill as a Goldman Sachs PAC event. This marks possibly the first time anyone has used Goldman Sachs as a PR cover.

Happy ending? Penny's gone, yes. But her poodle, Tim Geithner, and her policies, and the power of privilege, passed to Goldman, remain.

9.

One Thousand
$100 Bills

Neither Singer the Vulture, the Kochs, Penny P., nor the Ice Man invented the checkbook election.

In 1972, there was CREEP, the Committee for the Re-election of the President. The CREEP-in-Chief was Richard Nixon.

You probably know this story from the papers if you were around then, or from the movie, *All the President's Men,* about the Watergate break-in.

I got the story from one of the guys who funded the break-in and cover-up, a Chicago businessman. He told me about it over escargot at an exclusive members-only eatery high above Michigan Avenue on Chicago's Gold Coast.

I'd never eaten snails before except on a dare, and I'd never seen a garlic clove. Where I come from, garlic is a powder in a plastic shaker. You put it on pizza.

The businessman laid it all out. He'd dropped at least $50,000 in cash on Jeb Magruder, Nixon's slithery little deputy campaign director. The businessman wasn't a Republican, he wasn't a Democrat either. He'd been a communist then switched to a cynicalist. He'd learned from Karl Marx that there are those who produce wealth and those who spend it. He thought the choice was obvious.

Anyway, for Magruder the cash for CREEP wasn't a political contribution but an investment, and the creepier and more illegal the use of his money by the president's men, the better—they'd owe him big time. The returns were already coming in. The businessman, Harold Palast, my uncle, was given two tickets to the President's inaugural ball, one ticket for him and one for the hooker in a ball gown that the Republican Party placed in his limousine to escort him for the evening.

They threw in a federal charter to start a bank—before Magruder began his prison term.

(NB: And one other thing, that stuff about breaking into the Watergate to find evidence that Nixon's opponent got help from Castro in Cuba? Forget that bullshit. If that were true, Nixon wouldn't have tried to blame the break-in on the FBI—the FBI would have done it gladly—long-serving dirtbag J. Edgar Hoover was director until his death in the middle of that election year. The Cubans weren't looking for evidence; they were looking to *plant* evidence.)

I wasn't a journalist then, just a student at the University of Chicago, and Uncle Harold wanted to explain why my professor, Milton Friedman, was a schmuck. There was no such thing as a "free market"—it was very expensive, you had to fix the game, and fixing the game required fixing the dealers at the blackjack table, the politicians. Uncle Harold paid off cops on the beat, he paid off ward captains, and now he'd pay off the president. You pay to play.

Others were playing too. Dwayne Andreas of Archer Daniels Midland Company placed one thousand $100 bills on Nixon's desk in the Oval Office ($25,000 of it ended up in the bank account of the Watergate burglars). Andreas was wary of checks after he'd faced criminal charges for paying Nixon's *opponent* $100,000 four years earlier. (He beat the charges.) Andreas must have thought he would win sympathy at the Justice Department, which was then up to its keister in the Watergate conspiracy because ADM itself was directing its own little conspiracy fixing the international price of vitamin C.

Years later, ADM got into a bigger con: ethanol—fuel from corn—which sucked up $30 billion in US Treasury subsidies, most going to ADM. Andreas agreed with Uncle Harold's philosophy. "There isn't one grain of anything in the world that is sold in a free market," Andreas said, "Not one. The only place you see a 'free market' is in the speeches of politicians."

We never got a free market, but politicians got a free ride—on ADM's planes. Senate Majority Leader Bob Dole took twenty-nine rides on ADM's corporate jet for his 1988 presidential campaign (for which he was fined by the Federal Election Commission).

Dole, known as the "Senator from Ethanol," also took a $100,000 donation from ADM for his Better America Foundation. And what could be better for America than Bob Dole as president? The charity was in fact a front for Dole's presidential run, and the FEC hammered Dole with a fine for that too. Back in 2003, Dole had to shut Better America. Today, under *Citizens* and *Speechnow*, Dole's foundation could make America even Better by campaigning with the "charity" money.

Unfortunately for Dole, in 1996, he suffered from electile dysfunction, losing the presidency to Bill Clinton, a candidate generously funded by . . . ADM.

In 2008, the new "Senator Ethanol," Barack Obama of

Illinois, also earned a lot of frequent flyer miles on ADM planes jetting into Iowa during the presidential primary. (No FEC fine.)

While I don't approve of the president getting high with ADM, to his credit, I have to say that by 2012, Obama's budget zeroed out the subsidy for ethanol.

10

Target 67C

In May 1989, loaded with FBI reports and videotapes, the US Justice Department drafted this indictment under the Racketeer Influenced and Corrupt Organizations (RICO) antimobster law:

> Re: *************67C
> Koch Industries Incorporated
> Wichita, Kansas;
> CRIME ON AN INDIAN RESERVATION—
>   THEFT;
> RACKETEERING INFLUENCE AND CORRUPT
>   ORGANIZATION

Charles Koch wanted it all, and now, if federal prosecutors had their way, he'd get it: handcuffs and his Miranda rights.

But then he didn't get it all: that is, Charles and brother David got their $40 billion but no hard time.

Here's the draft of the indictment, or I should say, The Indictment That Never Was.

And who is "67C" whose name is blacked out, facing criminal charges?

. FD-?12 (i.. ... 12-9-77)

United States Department of Justice
Federal Bureau of Investigation
July 26, 1989

Honorable Robert Mydans
Interim United States Attorney
Western District of Oklahoma
Oklahoma City, Oklahoma

Attention: Nancy Jones
            Assistant United States Attorney

RE: 67C

            Koch Industries Incorporated,
            Wichita, Kansas;
            CRIME ON AN INDIAN RESERVATION -
            THEFT;
            RACKETEERING INFLUENCE AND CORRUPT
            ORGANIZATION

On page four, it says Assistant US Attorney Nancy Jones,

"after reviewing the facts of this case, stated it appeared to her at this time that there was reasonable and probable cause to believe that KOCH OIL COMPANY under the direction of [blacked-out and written-in by hand: "67C"] was engaged in corporate directed theft from Government lands and non-government lands, involving interstate pipeline, and from Indian country."

What the hell was going on? What happened to the criminal charges against Koch?

First, a key witness was bullied: Christopher Tucker gets a threatening visit from a security firm that worked for Koch Oil. Tucker, who won't break, contacts Assistant US Attorney Nancy Jones, who drafted the original indictment. Now she was considering drafting another charge, obstruction of justice, naming Koch Oil. The felonies were piling up.

Then, Jones had an accident: Senator Don Nickles.

Prosecutors serve at the pleasure of a state's US senators. And senators from Oklahoma and Kansas serve at the pleasure of the Kochs.

Using his senatorial privilege, Nickles had Tim Leonard, an oilman who did business with the Kochs, named US attorney for Oklahoma, making him Jones's boss. In 1992, Leonard pushed out Jones. The brilliant investigative reporter Bob Parry, who'd been sleuthing around the story a long time, discovered that—no surprise—Jones had to leave because the "political" fix was in on the Koch case, and she refused to roll over.

Jones's replacement disbanded the grand jury charged with investigating the Kochs without letting the jury even see the evidence compiled. Senator Nickles's handpicked prosecutor then wrote the Kochs, promising there would be no prosecution.

It looked like blue skies for the two Brothers Koch. But

they had two big problems: Charles and David's older brother Fred Jr., and David's twin brother Bill.

At Thanksgiving dinners, the Kochs are more likely to carve up each other than the turkey. David and Charles pushed elder brother Fred Jr. out of the family business. Then Charles helped David play a little con on David's twin, Bill, the dissolute playboy, to get Bill to fork over his share of his inheritance, his chunk of Koch Industries, for about half a billion dollars. Bill claims that half a billion was robbery because it didn't include the value of all the Koch monkey business. They sued each other, smeared each other, and rebuilt the New York State Theater in New York City so they wouldn't be seen as just a bunch of Wichita hayseeds. But they renamed the theater "Koch," which proves they still are.

During Koch-on-Koch warfare, documents and information made its way to the Senate Investigations Committee. The US Treasury, not just some Indians, had been ripped off by the oil skim on federal property. Moreover, messing with prosecutors got FBI agent Richard Elrod's knickers in a twist, and Agent Elrod started screaming about the vanishing indictment.

The committee's investigators had gathered enough evidence to burn Koch Industries and Senator Nickles from hell to breakfast.

But Nickles was the right wingman to the leader of the Senate's Republicans, Bob Dole. Hearings had already commenced when, in March 1990, Dole rose on the floor of the Senate to give what has got to be one of the most unusual statements ever made in that august hall: Dole launched into a passionate defense of an organization facing criminal indictment, Koch Industries, claiming they'd been victimized by liars. A lying videotape, I suppose.

Dole called Koch Industries a "solid corporate citizen," a citizen headquartered in Kansas, Dole's state. Remember that phrase: *"corporate citizen."*

In 1996, the lingering smell of it drew me to Wichita and then to Washington, DC. I figured some Democratic senator had the inside skinny and would blow the whistle. There was one ready to blow loudly: Senator Dennis DeConcini of Arizona.

The senator told me, "It was theft. We had hard evidence of theft." It was huge, he said, tens of millions worth of oil snatched from Indian and federal lands, possibly over $100 million pilfered altogether. It was the worst and biggest case of fraud against American Natives since Little Big Horn. And Senator DeConcini knew well that Prosecutor Jones had been yanked as punishment for bringing the racketeering indictment against Koch Industries.

DeConcini was going to go after them—but they went after *him* first.

DeConcini told me that the Kochs (the anti-Bill faction) sent an emissary who told him they would spend any amount of money to defeat and destroy him.

Threatening a prosecution witness is obstruction of justice. Threatening a senator on the Investigations Committee is what? Obstruction of democracy?

DeConcini didn't bend. He demanded further hearings and had every intention of hauling the Kochs in for questioning under oath.

But the hammer swiftly came down on DeConcini. He was named as one of the "Keating Five." The Senator had taken a $48,000 campaign contribution from banker Charles Keating, and met with regulators to get them off Keating's back. DeConcini was reprimanded by the Senate Ethics Committee and lost his Senate seat. (DeConcini's fellow senator from Arizona, John McCain, took $112,000 from Keating, plus free trips to the Bahamas, and a business deal for his wife, Cindy. But McCain plead stupidity to investigators, he said he had no idea what he was doing, and the committee found his defense credible.)

While Keating's cash to DeConcini was creepy but legal, not so the bigger bag of booty to the man who body-blocked the Senate investigation of Koch, Bob Dole.

The Kochs, big-hearted philanthropists, made a donation of $225,000 to the Dole Better America "Foundation."

Dole too had to give up his seat in the Senate—to accept

the GOP nomination for president. David Koch threw him a birthday party and gathered $150,000.

Hardly had the Kochs killed off the Indian and federal land-theft indictment when the company was charged with dumping three million gallons of murderously toxic oil residue into rivers in six states. This was followed by a ninety-seven-count criminal indictment.

Despite heavy pressure from Minority Leader Dole, this time the feds wouldn't budge.

So, if the Koch companies couldn't shake the law, they'd simply have to *change* the law.

Take note—this is a billionaire's favorite jingle: *if you can't do the time, make it no longer a crime.*

For the Kochs, changing the laws would be easy-peasy: all they had to do was flip Congress from Democratic to Republican, make Minority Leader Dole the majority leader of the Senate, and change the House leadership to something more crime friendly.

First, the Kochs would need to find a self-aggrandizing zealot with a spider-fast brain, a wandering weenie, and a heartless appreciation of the Kochs' self-serving ultra-right pseudo-libertarianism. A radical congressman from Georgia, Newt Gingrich, was known for whacky speeches to a completely empty House chamber, happy just to hear the echo of his own voice. With his Napoleonic self-regard and an inescapable scent of ethical ambiguity, Newt was the perfect front man for the Kochs' congressional coup d'état.

For Newt to seize Washington and rewrite laws for the Kochs, he'd have to put out a contract on their enemies.

So was born the "Contract with America." The Kochs, staying well hidden, used their cat's paws—"think tanks" like the Heritage Foundation, Cato Institute, and George Mason University—to draft the Contract with Newt. The Heritage Foundation had already been impregnated by the Kochs with $50 million and Cato seeded with $30 million. George Mason U got God knows how much from the brothers, because the school don't have to say.

Newt now had loads of money to jack up Republicans, but he wanted something in return, their signature on the Contract with America. Most interesting was Clause 7, the Job Creation and Wage Enforcement Act, which boosted the Regulatory Flexibility Act and decriminalized the Koch Brothers' poison-dumping. If passed, the expected criminal charges against Koch Oil would have to be dropped. The Center for Public Integrity commented, "This provision seems to have been drafted and designed for the Koch interests." Wrong. It was designed *by* the Koch interests.

But how the hell were super-rich wads like the Koch Brothers to get working-class voters to turn over the government to a megalomaniacal ponce like Gingrich? Answer: the way the rich have always done it—run candidates against the "plutocracy," the "elite," and yes, the "rich."

With their loot, the Kochs created a fake-o "populist" movement. To begin with, the Kochs purchased a not-for-profit group known for its antiestablishment, libertarian, get-the-hell-off-my-land views, the National Taxpayers Legal Fund, headed by Congressman Ron Paul of Texas. It was a weird corporate-style takeover. In 1984, the Kochs paid off the group's debts, changed its name to Citizens for a Sound Economy, and kept Paul on the Koch payroll as chairman of CSE until the day the Kochs had no further use of him. With CSE and other fronts in their holsters, the Kochs then funded a "grassroots populist" uprising that went under the name Wise Use Movement.

Two decades later, the Kochs used the same game to take over and fund a reprise of the Wise Use Movement. Wise Use morphed into the Tea Party. The Tea Party, which began out of true working-class anger over Washington plutocrats, was soon taken over and directed by the Washington plutocrats at FreedomWorks. FreedomWorks was the new name the Kochs gave their old Citizens for a Sound Economy. They didn't even bother to change the address or phone number. But they did rename the Tea Party platform as the Contract from America—which real Tea Party creators were not allowed to draft—referencing Gingrich's earlier initiative from the 1990s.

But back in 1996, there was no way the Kochs could buy a new Congress without some help from the Lord, diamonds, and cannibals.

11

Christians, Cannibals, and Diamonds

There is an Invisible Cord that connects the Gingrich coup that seized Congress for the GOP in 1994 to the cash flow in the election of 2012, most specifically Karl Rove's Incredible Bulk: the quarter billion for American Crossroads and Crossroads GPS. The Invisible Cord winds from Virginia Beach to the Congo, Washington, DC, and Liberia, a warlord madman with a child army, a super-model dumber than a sack of rocks (diamond rocks), and the Reverend Marion "Pat" Robertson.

This election year began with a YouTube video, *Kony 2012*, that went crazy viral. It was about Joseph Kony, the monstrous African warlord with an army of captive children. But Kony is a mere copycat killer, a bloody second-tier maniac compared to the inventor of the child army, Charles Taylor, sentenced in the Special Court of Sierra Leone in 2012 for multiple counts of murder, rape, and the use of child soldiers.

In Liberia, in 2010, I met one of these "soldiers": Peter Tah, a one-armed kid (there were many) selling chewing gum on the streets of the capital. Peter was nine years old when the warlord invaded his village, hacked his father to death with a machete in the family doorway, then told Peter they'd kill him if he didn't join their army. In three days, he was on the front line with an AK-47 bigger than he and was quickly shot in the arm. There was virtually no medicine in Liberia for saving his arm, so doctors had to amputate.

Charles Taylor, the Liberian warlord who holds the patent for inventing the first child army, is a cannibal, a mass murderer, and a credentialed economist—a much-too-frequent combination. He earned his degree in Massachusetts where he was later imprisoned for embezzlement, then escaped to Liberia and formed his kiddie army.

Taylor slaughtered his way into the presidency of Liberia where, in short order, he was facing arrest for crimes against humanity, including fomenting civil war in neighboring Sierra Leone so he could control the traffic in illegal "blood" diamonds. The evidence against him included his sending supermodel Naomi Campbell a little bag of diamonds-in-the-rough as an inducement to affection.

It didn't work: since they looked to Ms. Campbell like just a bunch of dirty pebbles, she gave them away.

But Taylor had a friend in God, or at least the Lord's sales rep on Earth, Dr. Pat Robertson. At Taylor's request, the Reverend Robertson spoke to President George W. Bush about backing off Taylor. Robertson said he spoke on the maniac's behalf as a matter of heavenly mercy, and it had nothing to do with Taylor's giving Robertson a gold mining concession.

(Note: While Robertson is called "Reverend" in the press, he, in fact, defrocked himself, leaving the Baptist Church. He told me he is *not* a televangelist, but a "businessman." Amen to that.)

Why would Bush listen to Robertson? What did Bush (and the Bush family) owe the Reverend Pat?

It goes back to that 1994 election and earlier.

In the Year of Our Lord 1994, as Newt was preparing his Contract with America, the Reverend Robertson raised millions to buy airplanes to feed the desperate survivors of the recent massacre in Rwanda. The reverend was filmed handing out food in the African refugee camps, then, when the cameras were turned off, he loaded the planes with equipment to take to the diamond mines he owned in the Congo.

The IRS, under a Democratic administration, was having trouble avoiding the smell of sulfur from Robertson's "not-for-profit religious" organizations which were making him a billionaire.

Either the law would end Robertson or Robertson would end the law.

The Lord heard Robertson's prayers and whispered, "Use the Lists."

The Lists: Three million names of the faithful donors to the not-for-profit religious educational group Christian Coalition. Political use of the lists was a crime. But there is a Higher Law—Reverend Pat's. So the Lists were given, in secret, to a convicted con man and traitor, Colonel Oliver North, the Republican candidate for Senator for Virginia. Members of the Christian Coalition received a message from the Lord: campaign literature announcing His endorsement for the crazed colonel for Senate.

While the Lists, not only from the Christian Coalition but from Pat Robertson's cable television "church," were put in the service of politicians, they also did service for mammon. Two insiders told me Robertson used his ministry to obtain millions in investments in the Kalo-Vita vitamin Ponzi scheme. Then he allegedly used the business lists as "an organizational structure to back his political agenda," that is, church assets were allegedly used in political campaigns—which was unquestionably illegal. *Then.*

In 1999, I was granted a rare audience with Dr. Robertson (that's another story) and the business director at his TV-studio-cum-church in Virginia Beach. I was nervous, constantly fondling my cigarette lighter. (I don't smoke—mild asthma—so I didn't bother putting fuel in the lighter: it enclosed a tiny tape recorder which the Rev. Pat's security crew allowed me to take through the metal detector.)

"The Doctor," as he prefers to be called, spoke to me at length in his television studio dressing room, slowly removing his makeup mask. What was underneath was most interesting.

In 1988, the Lord told Robertson to run for president. I asked how Robertson could have lost the presidential race with the Almighty as his campaign manager.

The answer was that the Lord wanted him to *run*, not win, and—*pay attention to this*—to create that three-million-name mailing list and political fist known as the Christian Coalition, which would forever give the Christian Right (i.e., Robertson) veto power over GOP candidacies. Of course, that wasn't legal. *Not yet.*

I learned more from my sources. On September 15, 1992, the Christian Coalition's President Ralph Reed told George Bush's campaign he was prepared to provide 40 million so-called "voter guides" that would in fact help Bush, "a virtually unprecedented level of cooperation and assistance . . . from Christian leaders." Unprecedented and illegal.

And strange in another way: Robertson had just a couple months earlier said that Bush was "unwittingly carrying out the mission of Lucifer." But if Satan could get reelected, it was unlikely He'd investigate the source of his reelection.

Judy Liebert, former chief financial officer of Robertson's godly empire, has allowed me to reveal her name. She told me she complained to Ralph Reed, Christian Coalition president (and today a big-shot Republican consultant), when he began destroying documents subpoenaed by the FBI. She said Reed told her, "Why don't you just take a gun and blow my brains out?"

Amen to that.

But Rev. Robertson had the last laugh: On March

26, 2010, the US Circuit Court of Appeals unlocked the monster in the box. In *SpeechNow.org v. Federal Election Commission* and *Republican National Committee v. FEC*, the court took the *Citizens United* case to its mad conclusion: not just corporations but not-for-profit groups could spend without limit on political campaigns. The Christian Coalition's tricks were now treats, and the abuses of Robertson's businesses for political purposes now became court-blessed uses.

While much attention has focused on *Citizens United* and allowing corporations to fund political campaigns, the *SpeechNow* ruling that followed blessed the greater danger: not-for-profit "social welfare" organizations, including Rove's Crossroads, their agendas obscured and their funding sources hidden.

But in 1999, the hour for these rough beasts was yet to come. Someone, someone who couldn't care less about no stinkin' lawmen's badges, had to lay the beastly seed for *Citizens United* and corporatocracy. That someone, or something, was named "Triad."

12.

The Hunt for Triad

In 1996, Bill Clinton cleaned Dole's clock in the presidential race. But, against all the odds, despite the crushing Democratic victory at the top of the ticket, Republicans under Gingrich kept control of the House.

Gingrich could thank the Coalition for Our Children's Future.

What was a bit odd about this group is that they didn't seem to give a shit about children. They were a tax-exempt "social welfare" organization. However, they weren't a charity raising funds for school lunches. The committee spent millions, but not one dime of it for anything to do with any children at all.

They did spend money on advertisements. The ads ran in seeming coordination with Citizens for Reform, whatever the hell that is, and Citizens United, a group that refused to identify any of the citizens who had united.

Every ad was a vicious attack on twenty-nine vulnerable Democrats running for Congress, all broadcast in the week or so before the election. They spent millions when a million bucks dropped into a campaign was atomic. For example, one ad linked a Democrat with a "child molester." Another told Montana voters that the Native American (and Democratic) candidate for the US Congress, Bill Yellowtail, was a "convicted felon" and a "wife-beater."

And in Kansas, voters were asked by fake "pollsters" if they would still vote for Democrat Jill Docking for the US Senate if they knew she was Jewish.

The Democrats, stunned by this attack from a secret source, had no time to respond to this bombardment of slanderous feces. The result was the upset defeat of at least a dozen Democrats, some by just two hundred votes, including Yellowtail and the "Jewess" Docking.

The Coalition for Our Children's Future was triumphant. What that meant for children's future was that Congress took a hatchet to food stamps for poor kids. You could say that the Committee for Our Children's Future and its cousin organizations changed forever the political face of our nation.

So, we're back to Butch's question to Sundance, "Who *are* these guys?"

The answer: Triad.

The director of Children's Future swore to congressional investigators that he was forced to sign over $700,000 in blank checks from an anonymous donor. Children's Future had signed confidentiality agreements with the donor.

It was Triad, a consulting firm named after the secret

Chinese money-laundering gangs, which had channeled the anonymous millions into Children's Future and its affiliates. If Children's was, in fact, not a real charity, nor Triad a "consulting" firm, but a money-laundering service for campaign spending by wealthy donors and corporations, then the list of felony crimes committed would make the Cosa Nostra blush.

There was more funny-money bending that campaign. In 1996, Citizens United took in donations from wealthy conservatives and sent them out, in the same amount and same day, to candidates who'd already received the legal maximum from their donors. It seemed a screamingly obvious route around campaign donation limits. But Citizens' lawyer said the payments' sums and timing were just a "coincidence."

Republican Senator Fred Thompson was chairman of the Committee on Governmental Affairs, which investigates corruption. Thompson thought of himself as a real crime-fighter, a tough federal prosecutor (though his biggest wins as an attorney were on the TV show *Law & Order*). He was truly upset that Citizens United, Children's Future, and all these front groups had stonewalled his requests for information. Nevertheless, on the evidence he could gather, he wrote a red-hot report that whoever was behind the money flow was guilty-guilty-guilty of:

"*disingenuous incorporation as a for-profit business and the establishment of sham nonprofit corporations. This secretiveness undermines our system of campaign-finance laws.... Triad is important not just for the ways it bent or broke existing laws, but for the pattern it has established for future groups, which will take comfort in Triad's successful defiance of this Committee.*"

Thompson then marched onto thin ice, laying out the circumstantial evidence that the money from Citizens United was a front for illegal excess contributions by ultraright billionaire Foster Friess—and, more threatening to the GOP, that Triad was an illegal conduit for money from Koch Industries.

Remember, these are the Olden Days before *Citizens United*. In the brave new post–*Citizens* world, Friess could openly give millions to a single candidate, the $2,000 limit be damned. (And he did. Friess blessed ex-Senator Rick Santorum in 2012 with millions to run for president and against condoms.)

But back in 1996, it was a crime

The Koch Brothers
Brothers Grim
Charles and David, the richest guys you've never heard of—net worth $6 billion.
Made their money the old-fashioned way, stealing from Indians. Koch oil company caught siphoning tanks on Oklahoma reservations.
Big-time philanthropists: Purchased U.S. Congress for Koch Industries. Through front called Coalition for Our Children's Future, secretly funneled millions into ads slandering Democratic candidates. It worked, putting Republican carnivore Newt Gingrich in charge of Congress.
• Every Republican elected with "Children's Future" cash voted to end food stamps for children—and boosted Gingrich's "Contract on America."
• Newt's "Contract" would let Koch Industries off the hook on criminal pollution charges.
Charles Koch: "I want my fair share, and that's all of it."

(Footnote: Want to play with a full deck? The Joker's Wild, tarot cards by Greg Palast. With billionaires and their politicians drawn by Bob Grossman. Visit www.BallotBandits.org.)

for corporations to give money to political campaigns: a breakin'-rocks-on-a-chain-gang, go-to-jail felony crime. So was excess or hidden giving to campaigns. Thompson was in the mood to let the Democrats draft subpoenas, compel testimony from the Kochs, and force the brothers to divulge their records. Wow.

I was intrigued by Thompson's burst of crazy-ass moral outrage and made a few discreet calls to a pro inside the committee operation.

Here's what I got: Nixon's chief of staff once called Senator Thompson "dumb as hell." Clearly, Thompson didn't understand the play, the GOP game plan. He'd been elected senator from Tennessee on the strength of his pretend "admiral's" rank in the film *The Hunt for Red October*. Thompson didn't need his party's fat cats, so he didn't care about the GOP's desperate need to cover up Citizens United's sleazy-squeazy or Koch's hot-money injections. The Republican leadership would set him straight. They took away his ability to issue subpoenas, but let him keep the perks of chairmanship, which included schtupping the Senate Republican's comely blonde legal counsel.

Republican leader Senator Trent Lott did the honors of putting a hammerlock on pretend lawman Thompson.

On December 31, 1998, Senator Thompson's Governmental Affairs Committee shut down its investigation into campaign finance shenanigans without having brought in key witnesses, failing even to subpoena key documents.

But why would the Democrats go along with letting the GOP's sugar-daddies off stone-free?

What the hell happened?

The answer, I was told: *Riady.*

13.

Manchurian Candidates

In 1996, Republicans were investigating President Clinton, that is, sniffing at his zipper and a wet cigar.

But I follow the money, not the semen. My target was an electric company, Entergy, one of Hillary Clinton's law clients whom I'd been tracking since 1985.[8] The Entergy money trail took me from Little Rock, Arkansas, to China, and right into the Oval Office. This was a hell of a lot more serious than an intern under the desk.

When Bill Clinton became president, Hillary's Little Rock client suddenly became a transglobal power-industry behemoth. Entergy bought the Indian Point nuclear plants in New York and the entire electricity system of London,

---

8   I was originally asked to investigate the company in 1981 by the attorney general of Arkansas, Bill Clinton. But I was a big-shot New York investigator with no interest in working for some small-time politician from Dawg Patch. Too bad: I could have put him on the straight path.

England. Its big score was to team up with the Riady family of Indonesia, ethnic Chinese billionaires with big plans to run the power systems of China.

But the Riadys and Entergy needed Clinton and his Commerce Secretary Ron Brown to grease up the Chinese for them, beginning with Brown taking Entergy bosses on a deal-making trip to China.

Secretary Brown was not pleased. According to his long-time business partner and love interest, Nolanda Hill. Brown fumed, "I'm not Hillary's motherfucking tour guide!"

The problem for the secretary was not the deed but the price. Brown, previously chairman of the Democratic Party, had enthusiastically endorsed a Hillary cash-for-access scheme: $10,000 for coffee with the president, $100,000 for a night in the Lincoln bedroom. But he resented the discount rate Hillary put on US executives joining Brown's own lucrative trade missions. The commerce secretary pouted, "I'm worth more than $50,000 a pop!"

But Brown had nothing to fear regarding his price: the Clinton campaign chest got a lot more than fifty thousand for the "pop."

Now follow this:

On June 22, 1994, the billionaire James Riady met with Webster Hubbell, former associate attorney general and Hillary Clinton's former law partner.

On June 23, Riady met with Hubbell for breakfast, then went to the White House, then returned to meet again with Hubbell, then made two more treks to the White House.

On June 26, videotape shows the beginning of a meeting in the Oval Office between President Clinton and Riady before the tape goes blank.

On June 27, Riady retains Hubbell as a consultant to Entergy.

How much advising Hubbell could do from prison, it was not clear.

At the time of his meetings with Riady, when he got his check, Hubbell was under indictment for fraudulently inflating his legal bills, a felony. He pled guilty.

Now, I've conducted investigations of lawyer over-billing. How can one law partner fake detailed time logs without the complicity of another lawyer in the firm? Hillary's logs were worth close inspection by authorities.

Funny thing about Hillary's billing records: when requested for disclosure in an unrelated matter, they disappeared. First, her law firm's computers went ka-blooey. Then the paper printouts vanished. But during the 1992 presidential campaign, just before the logs disappeared, her partner Web Hubbell secretly combed them over, line by line.

Hubbell knew his own logs were phony, and he understood the consequences of exposure: prison. Ultimately, the bloated hours on those records caused him to lose his law license, his Justice Department post, and his freedom—twenty-one months in the slammer.

What did Hubbell see and know about Hillary's own billing logs? Hubbell won't say, except for a cryptic remark, after seeing her bills, that "every lawyer" fabricates records. Does "every" include Hillary? Hubbell wouldn't say.

If he ratted out Hillary, he might have bargained himself an easy plea bargain. But Hubbell was a champ: silent.

Why would Hubbell choose to do time on the chain gang over testifying about Hillary? Could it be the $100,000 from the Riadys? (Altogether, Hubbell collected half a million dollars in the weeks up to his entering the slammer.)

Hillary's billing records finally reappeared, two years later, just outside her office, right after Hubbell's refusal to testify against her.

Maybe the Clintons knew nothing about the Riady money flowing to prison-bound Hubbell. Knowledge of the payments would suggest they were buying Hubbell's silence. That would be a criminal offense. An *impeachable* offense.

In notes I've obtained of the FBI's conversation with the president (who was under oath), Clinton first said he couldn't remember if Riady mentioned the $100,000 payment. Then, Clinton slyly opened the door to the truth, telling the agents, "I wouldn't be surprised if James told me."

Neither would I.

In all, James, his father, and Riady reps met with Clinton some ninety-eight times.

Four years after the Hubbell-Riady-Clinton meetings and payments, on December 31, 1998, Republican Senator Thompson's Governmental Affairs Committee shut down. They hadn't called the key witnesses against Clinton, and had issued no subpoenas for the key documents. Why? Why did the Republicans suddenly halt their inquiry into Clinton's fundraising just as they were closing in on the damning evidence?

It was the same day Chairman Thompson shut down the investigation of the Koch Brothers.

I could put two and two together. But just to make sure, I called the committee to confirm that two plus two made four. Sure enough, my insider, requesting anonymity, confirmed it was a secret straight-up deal between Republican and Democratic senators.

"A truce: You don't do Triad and we don't do Clinton [on Riady cash]."

PS: How did some unknown governor from the Podunk state rise like a rocket from Little Rock to the White House, zoom out of nowhere to become, in 1992, the nominee of the Democratic Party? But Bill Clinton didn't exactly come from nowhere: he came from the Democratic Leadership

Council. DLC Chairman Bill Clinton presided over this new caucus of conservative Democrats, and his nomination as the Democrat's presidential candidate ended half a century of control of the party by the tough-regulation philosophy of Franklin Roosevelt. Rather than FDR, the DLC's antigovernment rhetoric, its complaining about bureaucrats, rules, and regulations, echoed the philosophy of the Koch-funded Cato Institute.

And that's not surprising: the DLC was funded by $100,000 from the Koch Brothers.

Did the DLC investment pay off for the Kochs?

Once in the White House, Bill Clinton issued an Executive Order to force agencies to halt or roll back regulations based on costs to industry. Public health, welfare, and safety would no longer rule. The chief of Clinton's National Partnership for Reinventing Government, Vice President Al Gore, directed the antiregulatory attack with gusto, announcing he was "ending the era of big government." Gore created "regulatory partnerships," giving official review powers to executives of regulated industries. The Clinton-Gore administration radically slowed the movement to cap greenhouse gas emissions by heavily promoting a system of indulgences, "pollution credits," that allowed polluters to simply purchase the right to pollute. C. Boyden Gray, then head of Citizens for a Sound Economy, the lobby group founded by the Kochs, devised this "cap-and-trade" system.

In later years, the Kochs' Citizens for a Sound Economy

became FreedomWorks, the precursor of the Tea Party. The Kochs' chairman of FreedomWorks, that same Boyden Gray, is today leading the Tea Party crusade against "cap and trade," the pollution credit system created by . . . Boyden Gray. If you think that's a contradiction, you're not paying attention. The strategy of well-timed, stepwise manipulation of national policy debate evidenced here is nothing if not brilliant. The Kochs play an elaborate game of chess and we can't even see the board.

And did I say that the Kochs funded the rise of both presidential nominees, Clinton *and* his opponent, Bob Dole? Sure did. Billionaire Rule Number two: Don't bet on a horse when you can *buy the whole damn racetrack.*

■　■　■

But there was still the little matter of criminality. Riady money from Indonesia, Koch money through "Children's Future," fake-o foundations and political hit squads posing as think tanks, all this funny juice running through political arteries was, of course, illegal.

Illegal, that is, until 2010, until *Citizens United* and *SpeechNow.* For $200 and a post office box provided by a sketchy lawyer, the Riadys, the Zetas Gang Inc., British Petroleum, Qaeda Corp, Charles Manson LLC, and Vladimir Putin Partners can all incorporate and dump cash into US campaigns till their dark hearts are content. And so too the Christian Coalition and the Chinese politburo, giving a whole new meaning to the term "Manchurian Candidate."

One other thing: Just who are these "Citizens" that were "United" for Citizens United? How could this teeny group hire a supreme lawyer like Ted Olson to argue before the Supreme Court? Olson, former US solicitor general, doesn't work for peanuts. How could Olson keep body and soul together during this time-consuming litigation? Apparently he was given leave from his duties as legal counsel at . . . Koch Industries.

14.

Wyly Coyotes

In 2000, Republican presidential candidate Senator John McCain whupped Governor George Bush Jr.'s behind in the New Hampshire primary.

McCain didn't get to enjoy his victory very long. For the first time ever, a group organized under section 527 of the tax code could spend over $2 million crapping all over McCain on the airwaves. Who were the guys throwing the slime?

We now know it was the Brothers Wyly, two billionaires Charles and Sam who'd made a mint off a law signed by Governor George W. Bush of Texas deregulating the power industry (a law Sam helped write).

McCain's campaign was destroyed in the primaries when the Wylys targeted him, and that gave Governor Bush the presidential nomination.

A pissed-off McCain then joined with a Democrat, Russ Feingold, to shame fellow Congressmen into passing the Bipartisan Campaign Reform Act of 2002.

President George Bush decided to counter McCain and Feingold with a Highly Partisan Campaign Act, appointing in 2005 as chief justice of the Supreme Court a man who would thrill Bush's funders: John Roberts, corporate lawyer and probusiness fanatic.

Chief Justice Roberts set about immediately to aim his guns at McCain-Feingold. *Citizens,* which effectively demolished the McCain-Feingold Act, was a foregone decision.

But it wasn't good enough to demolish their act. The big money had to demolish Feingold and McCain.

With the 2010 decision chopping the head off his campaign reform law, Feingold's opponents were able to outspend him—extraordinary in a race by an incumbent—and Feingold lost reelection. The Number One contributor to Feingold's opponent? Sorry, no points for guessing this one either: Koch Industries.

And McCain? McCain saw the light and was born again, voting in 2007 against a law requiring disclosure of donors by lobbying groups—a law he himself proposed. And that 527 lobbying front for the Wylys that smeared McCain? The New McCain of 2008, the GOP presidential nominee, gave a speech to the group and took a big check.

McCain was trying hard to sell his soul to the Devil, but the Devil wasn't buying. Big Finance put its money on the new kid on the block, The One They'd Been Waiting For.

And adding insult to self-inflicted injury, McCain had

to return $20,000 to the Wylys. It later turned out much of the Wylys' money had been stolen, and in 2010, the Securities Exchange Commission whacked the brothers with charges alleging a half-billion-dollar ($550 million) fraud scheme that provided the grubstake for their billions.

15.

Karl Rove Confidential

Congressman Tim Griffin is a big, BIG supporter of the XL Pipeline. And the Kochs are big, BIG supporters of Congressman Griffin. Koch interests lined up $167,183 for Griffin's run in 2010. Let me put that in perspective: for $167,183, the average member of Congress would be willing to wash your car—with their tongue.

That kind of money doesn't come into a GOP candidate's hands without the helpful hand of Karl Rove.

If you remember, voting-rights attorney Kennedy said Griffin "should be in jail." A federal prosecutor expressed the same sentiment to me. How Griffin ended up in Congress, not in prison, is the more intriguing story.

It was well after midnight, some time in the first week of October before the 2004 election, when the e-mails started pouring in.

The chieftains of the George W. Bush reelection campaign were copying me on their most intimate and confidential messages—and Ollie, my research director, pissed me off by waking me in my cheap motel room to tell me this whacky-ass news. I was in the middle of nowhere USA with my election investigation for BBC going nowhere, so I wasn't in the mood for this bullshit.

But it wasn't bullshit. It was a miracle. Karl Rove's right-hand man, Tim Griffin, Bush's research director (read, *smear director*), had sent the data for some sick scheme to the chairman of the Bush reelection campaign in Florida, Brett Doster. Griffin, instead of sending copies to GeorgeWBush.com, their internal e-mail domain, sent copies to GeorgeWBush.*ORG,* to my friend John Wooden's joke site. Wooden passed them on to us for forensic analysis.

Here was the GOP leadership with their pants around their ankles, exposing their cheat sheets.

Holy Mama! Do I have to believe in God, now?

What we'd been handed proved to be an electronic back door into the darkest corners of a criminal vote-suppression machine.

By the morning, we had booked flights to Washington, DC, and Tallahassee, Florida, while Ms. Badpenny, in charge of our investigations, began the decoding work. We knew there was a scheme afoot, but what exactly was it?

Smoking-gun memos rarely read, "Louie, this is how we cheat the public," or "Brett, here's the plan to steal Florida." If they do say that, they're fake.

These e-mails' clues were a bit tougher than most to crack. That pudgy little wad Griffin had written to Doster several e-mails with the cryptic subject line *Caging.xls*, with Excel files attached, and terse messages like "Here's another list."

Each was a very selective list of voters, names, and addresses. What struck me right off were names like Rodriguez, Washington, and Goldberg—typically Hispanic, black, and Jewish. Badpenny and the crew mapped the addresses and, sure enough, it was a perfect scattergram of poor, minority neighborhoods and townships with *Gone With the Wind* names like "Plantation, Florida." There was also that list of Yiddish names from retirement homes: the GOP was certainly targeting the Elderly of Zion.

But for what?

At the Bush headquarters in Florida's capital, Campaign Director Doster agreed to an interview. But when BBC required me to disclose we had his "caging" e-mails, Doster fled like a bunny into his Tallahassee offices and sent out his mouthpiece, Mindy Tucker Fletcher, clutching a supersized cup of Coca-Cola as big as a mortar shell. She brought a flunky to nod at whatever she said, and a sneering list of explanations, beginning with a corker: the "caging" lists, she said, were a compilation of Republican donors.

Really? Including these folks? Here were the Bush-Cheney "donors" who all lived at the State Street Rescue Mission:

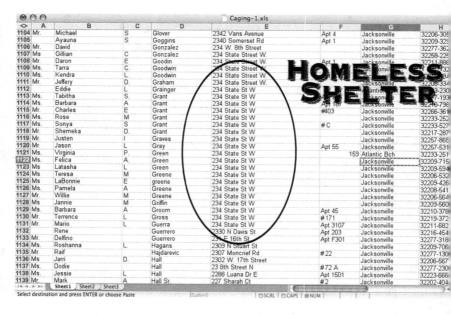

	A	B	C	D	E	F	G	H
1104	Mr.	Michael	S	Glover	2342 Vans Avenue	Apt 4	Jacksonville	32206-30ϟ
1105		Ayauna	S	Goggins	2340 Somerset Rd	Apt 1	Jacksonville	32209-32ϟ
1106	Mr.	David		Gonzalez	234 W. 8th Street		Jacksonville	32277-36ϟ
1107	Ms	Gillian	C	Gonzalez	234 State Street W.		Jacksonville	32258-22ϟ
1108	Mr.	Daron	E	Goodin	234 State Street W.		Jacksonville	3221ϟ-88ϟ
1109	Ms.	Tarra	C.	Goodwin	234 State Street W.	Apt 1	Jacksonville	ϟ3ϟ
1110	Mrs.	Kendra	L	Goodwin	234 State Street W.			ϟ3ϟ
1111	Mr.	Jeffery	D.	Graham	234 State Street W.			ϟ
1112		Eddie	L	Grainger	234 State St W		ϟantic	ϟ3-230
1113	Ms.	Tabitha	S.	Grant	234 State St W		ϟeon	ϟ7-193
1114	Ms.	Barbara	A	Grant	234 State St W	Apt 18ϟ	Jacksonville	3221ϟ-79ϟ
1115	Mr.	Charles	E	Grant	234 State St W	#403	Jacksonville	32266-36ϟ
1116	Mrs.	Rose	M	Grant	234 State St W		Jacksonville	32233-25ϟ
1117	Ms.	Sonya	S	Grant	234 State St W	# C	Jacksonville	32233-527
1118	Mr.	Shemeka	D.	Grant	234 State St W		Jacksonville	32217-287
1119	Mr.	Justen	I	Graves	234 State St W		Jacksonville	32257-865
1120	Mr.	Jason	L	Gray	234 State St W	Apt 55	Jacksonville	32257-531
1121	Ms.	Virginia	P.	Green	234 State St W		159 Atlantic Bch	32233-251
1122	Ms.	Felica	A.	Green	234 State St W		Jacksonville	32209-715
1123	Ms.	Latasha	L	Green	234 State St W		Jacksonville	32209-59ϟ
1124	Ms	Teresa	M	Greene	234 State St W		Jacksonville	32206-532
1125	Ms	LaBonnie	E	greene	234 State St W		Jacksonville	32209-426
1126	Ms.	Pamela	A	Greene	234 State St W		Jacksonville	32208-541
1127	Mr.	Willie	M	Greene	234 State St W		Jacksonville	32206-56ϟ
1128	Ms	Jannie	M	Griffin	234 State St W		Jacksonville	32209-560
1129	Ms.	Barbara	A	Groom	234 State St W	Apt 45	Jacksonville	32210-378
1130	Mr.	Terrence	L	Gross	234 State St W	# 171	Jacksonville	32219-372
1131	Mr.	Mario	L	Guerra	234 State St W	Apt 3107	Jacksonville	32211-682
1132		Rene		Guerrero	2330 N Davis St	Apt 203	Jacksonville	32216-454
1133	Mr.	Delfino		Guerrero	23ϟ E 16th St	Apt F301	Jacksonville	32277-318
1134	Ms.	Roshanna	L.	Hagans	2309 N Stuart St		Jacksonville	32209-706
1135	Mr.	Raif		Hajdarevic	2307 Moncrief Rd	#22	Jacksonville	32277-130ϟ
1136	Ms	Jarri	D.	Hall	2302 W. 17th Street		Jacksonville	32206-567
1137	Ms.	Dodie		Hall	23 8th Street N	#72 A	Jacksonville	32277-230
1138	Ms.	Jessie	L	Hall	2288 Luana Dr E	Apt 1501	Jacksonville	32223-666
1139	Mr.	Mark	A	Hall Sr.	227 Sharah Ct	#2	Jacksonville	32202-404

Sheet1 Sheet2 Sheet3

Select destination and press ENTER or choose Paste   Sum=0   SCRL   CAPS   NUM

Page after page of names contained residents of homeless shelters.

Want to try again, Mrs. Tucker Fletcher?

A "caging list," she explained, was a term of art in the junk mail business referring to returned letters. I knew that. The Republicans, she said, didn't want to send duplicates to wrong addresses.

You don't say! So Mindy, you're telling me that Karl Rove's top attack dog is now running the mailroom via confidential messages to state party chairmen—for *address corrections*?

Why don't I give you one more try, Mrs. Tucker Fletcher. Could these, by chance, be lists used to *systematically challenge the registrations of voters of color*?

Mindy Tucker Fletcher grinned and said, carefully, "This is not a challenge list. That's not what it's SET UP to do."

Bingo.

You see, we'd already made a couple of visits to experts before stopping by Fortress Bush. After sending the lists to America's junk mail king Mark Swedlund, who'd helped me on many an undercover investigation, I had a damn good idea what these were—an opinion confirmed, without prompting, by Ion Sancho, Florida's county elections supervisor, the recognized expert on voting systems—and vote heists. "They couldn't be anything but challenge lists. And if they are, they're breaking the law."

More than one law, actually, especially if the targets have a racial or religious profile. And it would be breaking a consent decree: years earlier, the Republican National Committee was caught challenging black voters en masse at polling stations and had promised, under penalty of perjury, not to do it again.

Now it looked like they were doing it again, but in a most sophisticated way. Bobby Kennedy explained the game: "They send out letters to poor black and Hispanic voters, first class, with instructions to return, don't forward, if the letter is not deliverable. The returned ["caged"] letter is then used as 'evidence' the voter's listed address is fraudulent, and the Republican functionary then gets the name struck from voter rolls, or the absentee ballot, if mailed in, is not counted."

Targeting the black, Hispanic, and Jewish vote this way is not just icky and racist, it's against the Voting Rights Act of 1965, which Kennedy's late father Bobby Sr., the US attorney general, and his uncle, President John Kennedy, helped draft. Bobby Jr., looking at the evidence, suggested hard time for Griffin and Rove.

CAGING: mailing to registered voters—soldiers, students, the homeless and others—and using "returned" letters to challenge their registrations and absentee ballots. SEAL Team Six members, it's November 2012: Do you know where your ballot is?

But who was going to prosecute Griffin and company, anyway? Was the Bush Justice Department going to tell Mr. Griffin, "spread'm?" Mr. Griffin, of the Bush campaign? Mr. Griffin, assistant to the senior advisor to President Bush?

16.

The Hysteria Factory

In early 2004, George Bush was not a popular president, what with wars and his billionaires leaving so little for the rest of us. But if malcontents, black folk, Latinos, and Jews lost their registrations, didn't get to vote, were *afraid* to vote, then swing states like New Mexico, Ohio, and Florida could be flipped.

A massive attack on voter rolls to remove names, to block voters from casting ballots, and challenging votes cast should do it. Millions of votes are made to disappear by stealth or just sheer incompetence, but Americans are too enamored of the television story of their democracy that they don't see it and won't hear of it.

The chairman of the US Commission on Civil Rights, Mary Frances Berry, told me, "Elections aren't stolen in the vote count—they're stolen in the *no* count," a thought perceptive enough to have her removed from the commission by President Bush.

Rove knows that to win in a nation where white voters were becoming the minority, the number of minority "unvotes" simply had to be goosed. Registry purges, ballot rejections, blocked voter drives, ID requirements, you name it: anything to block the voter or their vote was critical to the GOP. If Democrats had "Rock the Vote," Republicans would need to "Block the Vote."

Paul Weyrich, cofounder, with $50 million from the Koch Brothers, of the Heritage Foundation, while dining with Ronald Reagan, put it bluntly:

> "Now many of our Christians have what I call the goo-goo syndrome—good government. They want everybody to vote. I don't want everybody to vote. Elections are not won by a majority of people, they never have been from the beginning of our country and they are not now. **As a matter of fact, our leverage in the elections quite candidly goes up as the voting populace goes down.**"

And his "our" does not include those families in the State Street Rescue Mission.

Now, the best way to steal an election is to accuse the *other* guy of stealing the election. How else can you get Americans to tolerate the purge of thousands of African Americans from the voter rolls as criminals, to block Hispanic voters at the polls because they don't have citizenship ID, to throw out mail-in ballots because absentee voters used the wrong color envelope?

The answer: this bonfire of the ballot box—wrongfully purging half a million citizens, not counting 2.7 million ballots, and rejecting 2.9 million registrants—is supposed to *stop voter fraud.*

> *"Whether they admit it or not, the Democrats need lawbreakers such as illegal aliens—who are being illegally registered as Democrats—and killers, rapists, and robbers in order to increase their base of far-left voters."*

That's Mike Baker, Fox News, who spoke with my wingman Ronald Roberts (which isn't "Ronald's" real name, but we don't need every freak we are hunting Googling us).

Baker's canard of the mama-stabbing Mexican voter wave never stops quacking.

And that was Mindy Tucker Fletcher's last defense. I asked her, if the voters were not "caged" for the *purpose* of challenging, would the GOP still *use* the list to challenge these voters?

Well, of course. "You wouldn't want someone voting fraudulently, would you?"

No, I wouldn't, Mindy.

The GOP position is this: If the letters mailed to voters at their registration came back to the cage "undeliverable," that must mean this schemey voter was using a fake address so they could vote. Or vote twice. Fraud, mass fraud. There were tens of thousands of voters on these lists, so by Republican claims, a tidal wave of criminality.

Who were these fraudulent voters with fake addresses? Al-Qaeda stuffing the ballot box? The Zeta gang from Mexico? Castro's agents?

Badpenny went sleepless calling every number she could trace, starting with this GOP caging list:

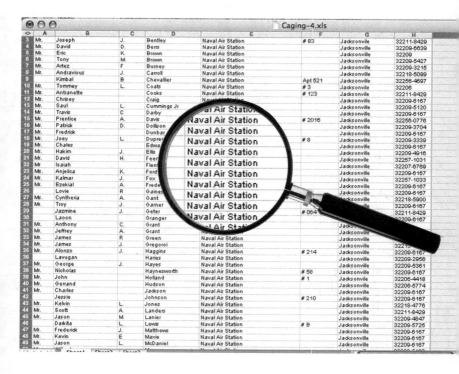

	A	B	C	D	E	F	G	H
3	Mr.	Joseph	J.	Bentley	Naval Air Station	# 83	Jacksonville	32211-8429
4	Mr.	David	D.	Berrs	Naval Air Station		Jacksonville	32209-6639
5	Mr.	Eric	K.	Brown	Naval Air Station		Jacksonville	32209
6	Mr.	Tony	M.	Brown	Naval Air Station		Jacksonville	32209-5427
7	Mr.	Artez	F	Burney	Naval Air Station		Jacksonville	32209-3215
8	Mr.	Andravious	J.	Carroll	Naval Air Station		Jacksonville	32218-5099
9		Kimbal	B	Chevallier	Naval Air Station	Apt 521	Jacksonville	32256-4697
10	Mr.	Tommey	L.	Coats	Naval Air Station	# 3	Jacksonvile	32206
11	Ms.	Antranette		Cooks	Naval Air Station	# 123	Jacksonville	32211-8429
12	Ms.	Chrisey		Craig	N		Jacksonville	32209-6167
13	Mr.	Saul	L.	Cummings Jr	Air Station		Jacksonville	32209-5120
14	Mr.	Travis	C	Darby			Jacksonville	32209-6167
15	Mr.	Prentice	A.	Davis	Naval Air Station	# 2016	Jacksonville	32256-0776
16	Mr.	Patrick	D.	Dollison	Naval Air Station		Jacksonville	32209-3704
17	Mr.	Fredrick		Dunbar	Naval Air Station		Jacksonville	32209-6167
18	Mr.	Joey	L.	Dupre	Naval Air Station	# 8	Jacksonville	32209-3339
19	Mr.	Chales		Edwa	Naval Air Station		Jacksonville	32209-6167
20	Mr.	Hakim	J.	Ellis	Naval Air Station		Jacksonville	32209-4916
21	Mr.	David	H.	Feer	Naval Air Station		Jacksonville	32257-1031
22	Mr	Isaiah		Flen	Naval Air Station		Jacksonville	32207-6769
23	Ms.	Anjelica	K.	Ford	Naval Air Station		Jacksonville	32209-6167
24	Mr.	Kalmar	J.	Fox	Naval Air Station		Jacksonville	32257-1033
25	Mr.	Ezekial	A.	Frede	Naval Air Station		Jacksonville	32209-6167
26		Lovie	R	Gaines	Naval Air Station		Jacksonville	32209-6167
27	Ms.	Cyntheria	A.	Gant	Naval Air Station		Jacksonville	32218-5900
28	Mr.	Troy	J.	Garner	Naval Air Station		Jacksonville	32209-6167
29		Jazmine	J.	Geter	Naval Air Station	# 064	Jacksonville	32211-8429
30		Laoon		Granger	Naval Air Station			32209-6167
31	Mr.	Anthony	C.	Grant	Air Stat		Jacks	
32	Mr.	Jeffrey	A.	Grant			Jacksonville	
33	Mr.	James	R	Green	Naval Air Station		Jacksonville	
34	Mr.	James	J.	Gregoroi	Naval Air Station		Jacksonville	3221
35	Mr.	Alonzo	J.	Haggins	Naval Air Station	# 214	Jacksonville	32209-6167
36		Lavugan		Haries	Naval Air Station		Jacksonville	32209-2956
37	Mr.	George	J.	Hayes	Naval Air Station		Jacksonville	32209-5361
38	Mr.	Nicholas		Haynesworth	Naval Air Station	# 58	Jacksonville	32209-6167
39	Mr.	John		Holland	Naval Air Station	# 1	Jacksonville	32206-4416
40	Mr.	Gerrand		Hudson	Naval Air Station		Jacksonville	32206-5774
41	Mr.	Charles		Jackson	Naval Air Station		Jacksonville	32209-6167
42		Jessie		Johnson	Naval Air Station	# 210	Jacksonville	32209-6167
43	Mr.	Kelvin	L.	Jones	Naval Air Station		Jacksonville	32218-4776
44	Mr.	Scott	A.	Landers	Naval Air Station		Jacksonville	32211-8429
45	Mr.	Jason	M.	Lanier	Naval Air Station		Jacksonville	32209-4847
46		Darkita	L.	Lewis	Naval Air Station	# B	Jacksonville	32209-5725
47	Mr.	Frederick	J.	Matthews	Naval Air Station		Jacksonville	32209-6167
48	Mr.	Kevin	E	Maxie	Naval Air Station		Jacksonville	32209-6167
49	Mr.	Jason	L.	McDaniel	Naval Air Station		Jacksonville	32209-6167

Page after page of felonious voters registered at the Naval Air Station in Jacksonville! How evil is that?! Using our own military as a cover for massive vote fraud!

Unless, of course, there was another reason why the seamen and airmen weren't at home. Badpenny reached one family and asked for the voter.

"Randall's been posted overseas," said Mrs. Prausa of her soldier husband.

Oh.

Active military may vote absentee from their US home address. But if GOP functionaries challenge them, their mail-in ballot is rejected—and they don't even know it.

Go to Iraq, lose your vote. Mission accomplished, Mr. Bush.

Indeed, I went through the lists with experts including Ion Sancho, the elections supervisor. He was getting more and more steamed. Who were the supposed fraudsters? Homeless men who don't have a name on a bell. Students away at school. Folks who move within their congressional district. And the 20 percent of US voters whose addresses contain typos from entries made by state employees into registry computers.

Every scheme to wipe away the voting rights of a US citizen, every legitimate ballot thrown in the garbage, every legal voter told to scram from the polling station, every diseased means used to defraud the public of the right to vote was justified by the hysterical claim of "VOTE FRAUD"!

But in all fairness, as a journalist, I had to look into the evidence of voter fraud. So I spoke personally with the attorney general of Florida.

The lawman, Bob Butterworth, assured me that if he found an illegal registrant or voter, he would arrest them, jail them. After all, an illegal voter, simply by the act of registering, had committed (another) felony.

I reminded him that Katherine Harris had found over ninety-one thousand illegally registered felons.

How many arrests had he made from her list?

"None." *Zero. Bubkiss. Nada.*

I don't get it. Busting them would be easy: After all, *we have their addresses on the registrations.* And they show up at the polls.

How many cases of vote fraud on that list?

"We've opened maybe half a dozen cases," the Florida AG told me.

Six out of ninety-one thousand???!!!

And it turns out those six charges were in error and dropped. Fraudulent voters: zero.

And the tens of thousands of caged voters? *Hundreds of thousands* caged by the GOP nationwide? If they were fraudulent voters, why weren't the jails filled with these felonious villains?

Because, says Dr. Lorraine Minnite, there is effectively no voter fraud in the US. Minnite, a professor at Rutgers University who actually dug into the crime files, discovered six—*six!*—convictions of vote fraud a year among 170 million voters.

Here's your crime wave: Over the entire study period, there were *two* convictions per year for multiple voting, two noncitizens, and two felons. (They must be the *dumbest* felons ever, willing to go back to prison just to vote for a school bond.) And that voter ID thief? Doesn't exist.

The truth is it's murderously hard to convince folks to register or vote illegally when it's absurdly easy to get caught and the penalty is long-term prison. Santiago Juarez, who runs voter drives in Mexican American neighborhoods, told me, "How do you organize thousands of people to vote twice? Hell, it's hard enough getting people to vote *once*." Stealing an ID to vote twice ain't happening.

Professor Minnite summed it up: "The claim of widespread voter fraud is itself a fraud." In 2012, over five million US citizens will lose their right to vote to prevent a crime committed by twelve individuals.

And the real criminals who are guilty of a couple million counts of violations of the Voting Rights Act, they're on Fox and PBS or in Congress, aren't they, Mr. Griffin?

17.

Tears of a Clone

In May 2007, BBC television led the nightly news with my report on new US Attorney Griffin and the "caging" of US soldier voters.

By the next morning, Griffin resigned and turned in his lawman badge.

While the BBC report was, as usual, ignored by US media, it wasn't ignored by the chairman of the House Judiciary Committee. Congressman John Conyers reached me in London to tell me he would subpoena Griffin.

Griffin held a truly weird press conference, bellyaching about "that British reporter," bursting into tears, and, despite the fact that his name was on the e-mails sending out the caging lists, he insisted, "I never heard of 'caging.'"

Really?

No one believed him. No one but me.

If he didn't send out caging lists, *who did*? Who would viciously, criminally, attack the rights of soldiers and homeless and old Jewish grandmas?

"Caging" is a technical term used in the direct mail business. So, who knows the direct mail biz and could use Griffin's personal computer?

Griffin's boss, Rove, knows about "caging." A lot. He became rich as owner of a direct mail company and was, in college, the CREEP computer whiz-kid who first introduced computer database mining in politics for Richard Nixon.

And he's infamously careful never to use his own computer.

So who used your computer, Tim? And then made you resign as prosecutor, shut up about the facts . . . and get the Kochs to buy you a seat in Congress?

Conyers told me he had loads of questions about this for Mr. Rove—who simply ignored the congressman's subpoena.

So we'll never know if the creep who sent out the caging lists was Karl Rove, his Rove-bot Griffin, or, a third possibility, Griffin's own gofer, Matt Rhoades.

While Griffin is now an Honorable Congressman (or, at least, a congressman), at the time, his career, following the BBC exposé, appeared to be toast. Indeed, John McCain dumped a high post for Griffin in his 2008 presidential campaign after the caging connection was made public.

But there is redemption. In 2012, Griffin's gofer, Matt Rhoades, was named director of the Romney presidential campaign.

18

A Few Good Men (Very Few)

Bobby Kennedy may think that Griffin's scheme to remove legal voters from the rolls was illegal, but Bush's Justice Department was not likely to bust one of their own.

Nevertheless, Griffin wasn't taking any chances. Neither was his boss, deputy chief of staff to the president and consigliere to the Bush reelection campaign, Karl Rove.

They feared there might be honest federal prosecutors. They could cause problems with The Plan to cage and challenge voters in 2004, in 2008, and beyond.

So, a directive came down from Main Justice in Washington to federal prosecutors nationwide: hunt for fraudulent voters. However, the lawmen were not told about an unwritten footnote to the directives: unsuccessful hunters would soon find themselves hunted.

I too was hunting for fraudulent voters—a good journalist

should give evil the benefit of the doubt. So I went to New Mexico to bag myself a killer-rapist-illegal-alien-ID-thief voter.

But I was having a helluva time finding even one, despite three million having lost their vote to prevent this terrible crime.

But then, in October 2008, a state legislator in New Mexico, Justine Fox-Young, held up two pieces of paper in the capitol building showing, she said, twenty-eight cases of someone voting with someone else's name. It wasn't a crime wave, but a kind of gentle ripple. So I called her and told to her to fax me the evidence. She didn't. I called again and asked the crime-buster politician, "Justine, you've uncovered felony criminals."

"Oh, yes!"

Cool. So did she turn over these villains to the federal prosecutors?

Uh-huh.

So, did the prosecutor arrest them? Lock'm up?

"Not *exactly.*"

The answer was, not even *remotely.* I called the federal prosecutor, a rising star in the Republican Party, US Attorney David Iglesias. He found Ms. Fox-Young's evidence just a load of bollocks, though he didn't use those words, I'll admit.

Iglesias hadn't arrested one single person in the entire state for voter fraud, despite the fact that the GOP campaign to prevent "fraud" in the state had resulted in the rejection of twenty-eight thousand voters and ballots, almost all Democrats.

In other words, the guy in charge of enforcing the law had not and would not bust a single person for the crime that justified his party's pogrom against Hispanic voters all across the Southwest.

I wasn't the only one to note that Captain Iglesias (he had remained in the Naval Reserve as one of the Navy's top adjutant generals) was not busting Bad Voters.

Around the same time, I discovered that Allen Weh, chairman of the state Republican Party, and Pat Rogers, the party's lawyer, complained to the White House about Iglesias failing to cuff these Hispanic voters after sending him fifty names, likely from the caging lists.

In 2008, Iglesias was able to tell me he "ran all over the plateaus of New Mexico with FBI agents" tracking down these fraudulent voters and found nothing but good citizens.

That wouldn't do for the party apparatchiks.

The Republican Chairman Weh, and his counsel, Pat Rogers, brought in an enforcer from the White House: Karl Rove.

In my line of business I hear a lot that could make you shiver, but what Captain Iglesias told me that day in 2008 was one of the most chilling things I'd ever heard from a US official.

The GOP honchos, state and federal, he said, wanted

him to *lock up voters no matter the evidence.* They wanted him to indict innocent people to justify their vote-blocking laws.

Iglesias told me, "I didn't help them with their bogus fraud prosecutions."

Rove's buddies leaned on Iglesias, but they picked the wrong guy. Captain Iglesias was one of the models for the Tom Cruise character, the crusading military defense lawyer, in the film *A Few Good Men.* Here's a photo of the pretend Iglesias, though more than a few women believe the real one is handsomer.

The real Iglesias told the Rove-bots to stick their phony prosecution demands where the votes don't shine.

So, President Bush fired Iglesias. And he wasn't the only one. Seven other US attorneys, good Republicans but ethical ones, were removed by the White House and replaced by pliant Rove-bots.

At first, the US press didn't notice. Iglesias was officially fired for "absenteeism"—because he was placed by the president on active duty and sent to Bosnia to address war crimes.

The press asked no questions, but one of my fans did when he watched my London broadcast on caging for BBC. Congressman John Conyers has always kept abreast of our investigations for BBC television. Conyers called me, then called hearings. He had plenty of evidence that the firings were illegal.

But the problem, Conyers told me, was that his fellow congressmen wouldn't go after the real issue, the motive for the firings: suppressing the vote of minority citizens. Conyers, dean of the Congressional Black Caucus, had the problem that while he was chairman of the House Judiciary Committee, the majority of them were Republicans or other members of the Congressional "White" Caucus.

The committee would concentrate only on the firings as "political," and a repeat-a-press-release US media covered it that way, never getting to the real motive. And most important, the Bush White House stonewalled Conyers' subpoena for cage-meister Griffin's boss, Karl Rove.

Conyers forced Griffin's cronies at the Justice Department to cough up their files on Iglesias's firing which included this smoking pistol:

Iglesias–Underachiever in very important district. That's the failure to bust innocent voters.

Absentee landlord. That's his forty-day assignment for the Navy. Firing reserve officers on active duty is a crime, but hell, that's nothing compared to the next felony on the list.

Domenici says he doesn't move cases. This is Republican Senator Pete Domenici who, said Iglesias, woke him up at home to tell Iglesias to speed up the indictment of a Democrat prior to the election.

Oops. He's telling a United States attorney to indict citizens, and attacking his failure to "move" when the Senator tells him too.

I asked the prosecutor if Rove had him removed as punishment for not bringing the fake cases. "If his intent was, 'look what happened with Iglesias,' if that was his intent, he's in big trouble. That is *obstruction of justice*, one classic example."

Iglesias was screwing them bad. The captain and eight other prosecutors were getting all precious about bringing bogus cases. That was undermining the GOP's attempt to obtain new voter ID laws. The failure to find illegal voters put the lie to their campaign to prove the nation's top voter registration organization, ACORN (Association of Community Organizations for Reform Now), had registered fraudulent voters. Getting ACORN was Republican operative Pat Rogers's obsession, which he made into a national cause of the GOP and other politicians in the White

Caucus as lawyer for the "nonpartisan" American Center for Voting Rights. It should have been called, American Center *Against* Voting. Everything the group proposed would cut the number of citizens voting by millions.

I wanted to ask Rogers why he brought in Rove and why he had Captain Iglesias gunned down. But Rogers didn't want to answer my formal request for BBC TV. But I figured he couldn't pass up the free champagne they would pour at a GOP victory party. At the soiree to which I obtained press credentials under another name, I caught Rogers in half-sip with an unseen microphone that captured his personal reviews of my reporting skills. "He's an asshole," he told a crony before greeting me warmly as the cameras rolled.

"Iglesias was not capable in his job." Which was, apparently, hunting ACORN.

"ACORN hired a collection of people who fraudulently registered persons who are not eligible to vote. ACORN is working for the Democratic Party," said Rogers. (He wore a flag lapel pin the party handed to all the champagne sippers. They gave me one of the Republican freebie flags. I still have it in the wrapper. Take a look: *Made in China.*)

Had Rogers unmasked a conspiracy between ACORN and the Democratic Party—covered up from them by US Attorney Iglesias, a Republican? Wow!

"Conspiracy," said Rogers mysteriously, "is a loose word." Rogers is fond of loose words. He'd recently held a press conference waving a list of a half-dozen fraudulent voters registered by ACORN. With his full house of illegal voters, Rogers made a huge splash in the papers. Then Iglesias made a total ass out of Rogers, by not busting even one.

What the hell, even a jerk reporter like me will give Rogers a chance. I checked out all six of these ne'er-do-wells, these fugitives from justice. I began at a diner in Cerritos where I tracked Melissa Tais, notorious for allowing another voter with another signature to use her name so she and her confederate could vote twice.

Actually, what she'd done was fill out one registration form at an ACORN table, but never received the receipt. So, following the law's requirements, she reregistered, this time signing while holding the form in her hand so the signature was a little shaky—resulting in two admittedly different-looking signatures.

So, did she vote twice? No. County officials hauled her into a hearing and it shook her up so much she wouldn't vote *at all*. And that's what they wanted.

But Iglesias wouldn't play and ACORN continued to register Hispanic and low-income voters until 2009, when Andrew Breitbart (who has since returned to the bosom of Satan) blew up some cockamamie sting which had nothing to do with voting—and put ACORN out of the registration business. (ACORN's one-time lawyer, Barack

Obama, averted his gaze as the media jackals savaged the poor folks' group, then paid for his pusillanimity in 2010 when Congress flipped color from Blue to Red.)

The US attorney firings occurred just in time for the 2008 election. Iglesias wasn't alone, of course. Tom Heffelfinger, Republican US attorney for Minnesota, was on the hit list for defending Native American voters from an attack by the GOP's Minnesota secretary of state. Iglesias called his buddy in Arkansas who was taken down for similar pangs of conscience, but agreed to step aside without a fight so his friend, President Bush, could make his own choice.

And Bush's choice was . . . *Tim Griffin.*

Elston, Michael (ODAG)

From:	Tim Griffin [griffinjag@comcast.net]
Sent:	Monday, February 05, 2007 8:09 PM
To:	Goodling, Monica
Subject:	I have one more or so.

Importance: High

That guy is a British reporter who accepted some false allegations and made a story up. That's why no other national press picked it up in 2004. Now Palast (who wrote about it the first time in 2004) has written about it again. It is all about an election year.

The RNC was in no way trying to keep anyone from voting.

D
w ...of the 2004 presidential campaign when Mighty Mouse, Donald Duck, etc. were registering to ...That was the context.

1

Elston, Michael (ODAG)

From: Tim Griffin [griffinjag@comcast.net]
Sent: Monday, February 05, 2007 8:07 PM
To: Goodling, Monica
Subject: HERE IS THE GREG PALAST ARTICLE
Importance: High

HERE IS THE ARTICLE THAT GREG PLAST WROTE THIS SUMMER: he h...
variations on the same theme. google bbc caging and greg palast and ...
charges against me and the RNC.

HERE IS THE LINK:

Now, instead of being prosecuted for crimes, Tim became the prosecutor. At Karl Rove's behest, Tim Griffin was appointed US attorney for Arkansas.

19.

The Purge'n General

Maybe you fall asleep reading pulp fiction, but I like to read tables of statistics. Unfortunately, this one popped me wide-awake: the US Election Assistance Commission's Annual Report.

(President Bush's Senior Advisor Mr. Rove created the Federal Election Assistance Commission as a supposed way to prevent "another Florida." When Rove and Bush tell you they want to "assist" your elections . . . well, you get the joke.)

A page-long table in teeny-weeny type, titled *Voter List Maintenance: Removal Actions*, listed the fifty-six states (don't forget the Virgin Islands, DC, Samoa, etc.), showing the number of names scrubbed by each secretary of state, a digit followed by a dot and a digit: Wyoming 4.5 percent, South Dakota 5.4 percent, and so on. But one state stuck out, literally, like an inflamed pimple, with its extra digit: Colorado: 19.4 percent.

That had to be a typo. If not, that meant that the secretary of state, Republican Donetta Davidson, had removed

19.4 percent or nearly one in five voters from the voter rolls. I checked the raw data and checked again. Yes, nearly half a million voters had been made to vanish with the stroke of the DELETE button.

Boy, is Katherine Harris going to be jealous when she hears about this.

And Colorado is the swingin'-est swing state there is. The pundits watched the state swing from 2008 Democratic victory to a Republican landslide in two years. The pundits gassed on about the Tea Party. Nothing about the voter lists.

I called the secretary of state's office for confirmation of numbers and an interview. No one would return my calls.

Maybe they had phone line trouble. So I flew to Denver with the voter roll info in hand and evidence I'd gathered from the clerks' offices in several counties (thanks to the help of a team on the ground led by Claudia Kuhns of the Public Integrity Project), and went to the office of the secretary of state. Where I was locked out.

I called the secretary of state's PR flunky on my cell.

"Greg Palast here. *Rolling Stone* and BBC TV. Listen, I'd love to speak with the secretary, or with you or with *anyone* who can explain what's going on here with these voter rolls."

Click. I wasn't even allowed up the elevator.

Since I'd already burned up my frequent flyer miles to get to Denver, I stopped by the office of Paul Hultin. He

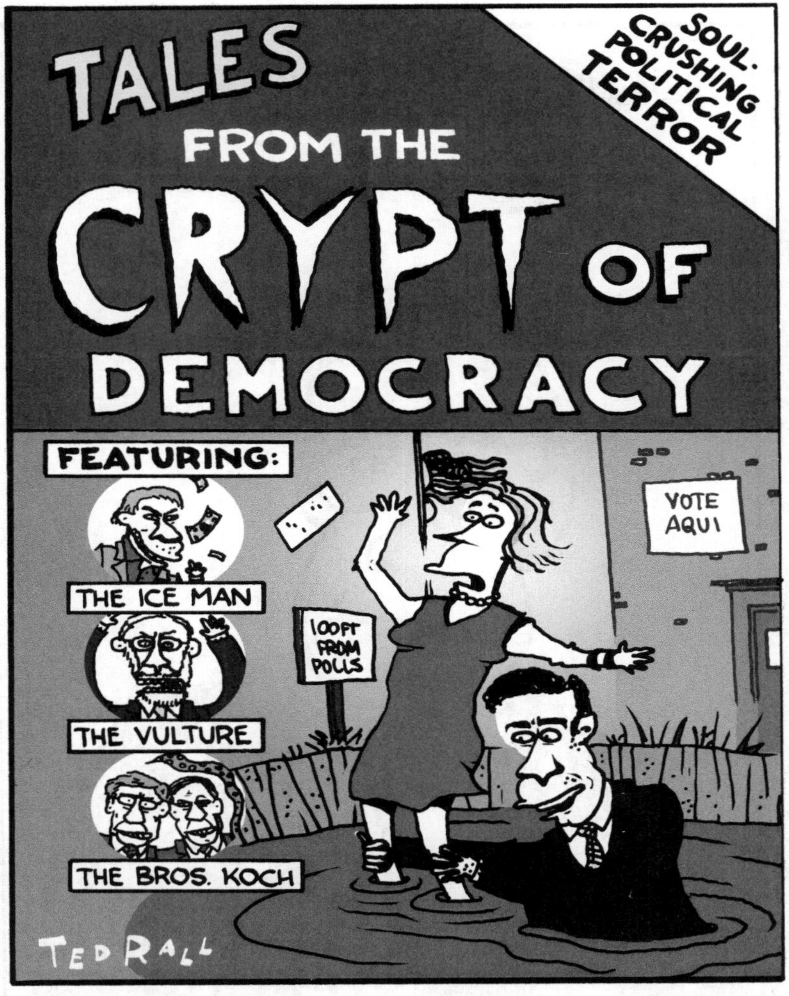
TALES
FROM THE
CRYPT OF
DEMOCRACY
SOUL-CRUSHING POLITICAL TERROR
FEATURING:
THE ICE MAN
THE VULTURE
THE BROS. KOCH
100FT FROM POLLS
VOTE AQUI
TED RALL

FROM BILLIONAIRES AND BALLOT BANDITS
A GREG PALAST INVESTIGATION
WWW.BALLOTBANDITS.ORG

REMEMBER KARL ROVE?

YOU TRIED TO FORGET "BUSH'S ARCHITECT."

Why Obama Is Likely to Lose in 2012.

KARL ROVE

Op-eds on *The Wall Street Journal's* right-wing editorial page

Attack ads by Rove's Crossroads GPS Super PAC

Harry Reid. <u>Extremely</u> out of touch with Nevada

FORGET FORGETTING.

HE'S BAAAAACK!

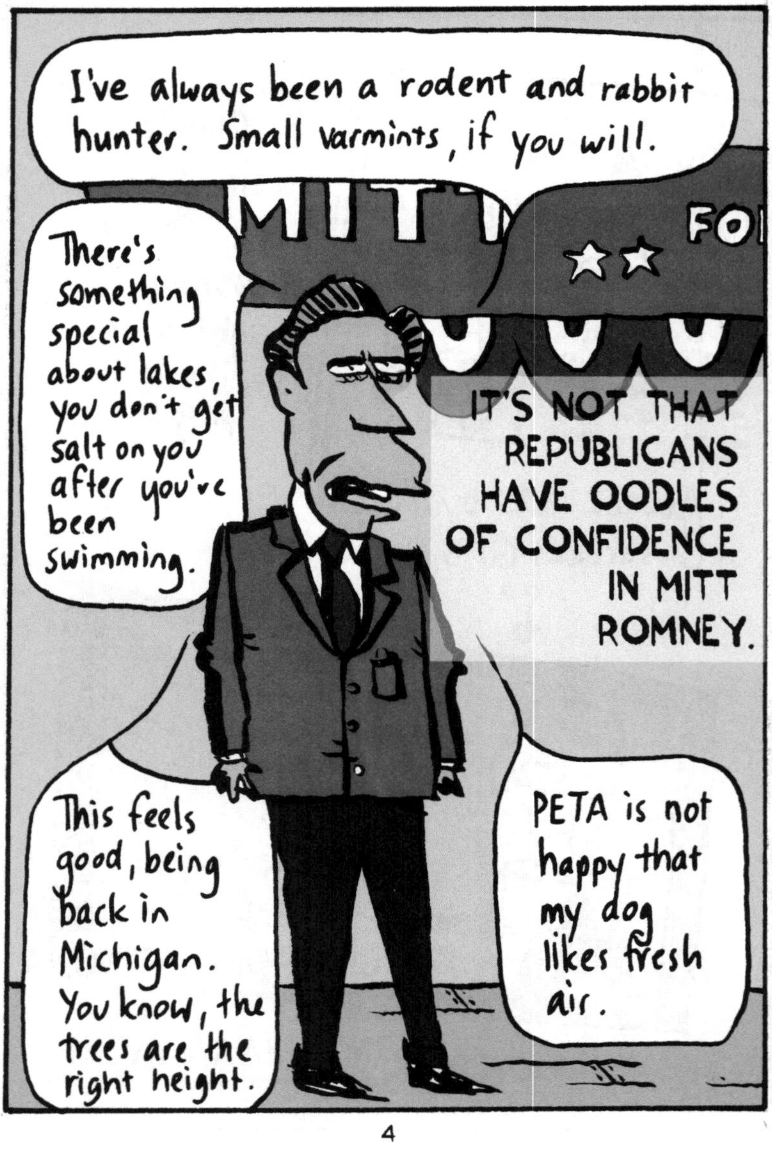
I've always been a rodent and rabbit hunter. Small varmints, if you will.
MITT
FO
There's something special about lakes, you don't get salt on you after you've been swimming.
IT'S NOT THAT REPUBLICANS HAVE OODLES OF CONFIDENCE IN MITT ROMNEY.
This feels good, being back in Michigan. You know, the trees are the right height.
PETA is not happy that my dog likes fresh air.

BUT THEY DO HAVE FAITH IN DIRTY TRICKS.

"If their [black voters'] share of the turnout drops just one point in North Carolina [in 2012], Mr. Obama's 2008 winning margin there is wiped out two and a half times over."

5

AS RECENT ELECTIONS HAVE PROVED,
THE GOP IS DAMNED GOOD AT KEEPING
BLACK PEOPLE AWAY FROM THE POLLS.

2004, OHIO

VOTE

LONG LINES AT POLLS IN BLACK DISTRICTS

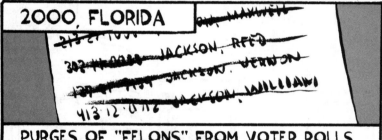

2000, FLORIDA

PURGES OF "FELONS" FROM VOTER ROLLS

2000, FLORIDA

POLLS

HOLO-
GRAPHIC
ID,
PLEASE.

GOONS QUESTIONING BLACK VOTERS

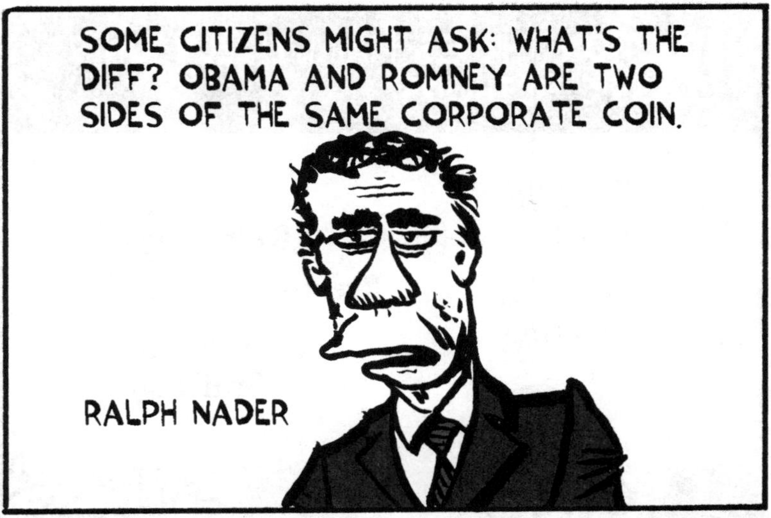
SOME CITIZENS MIGHT ASK: WHAT'S THE DIFF? OBAMA AND ROMNEY ARE TWO SIDES OF THE SAME CORPORATE COIN.
RALPH NADER

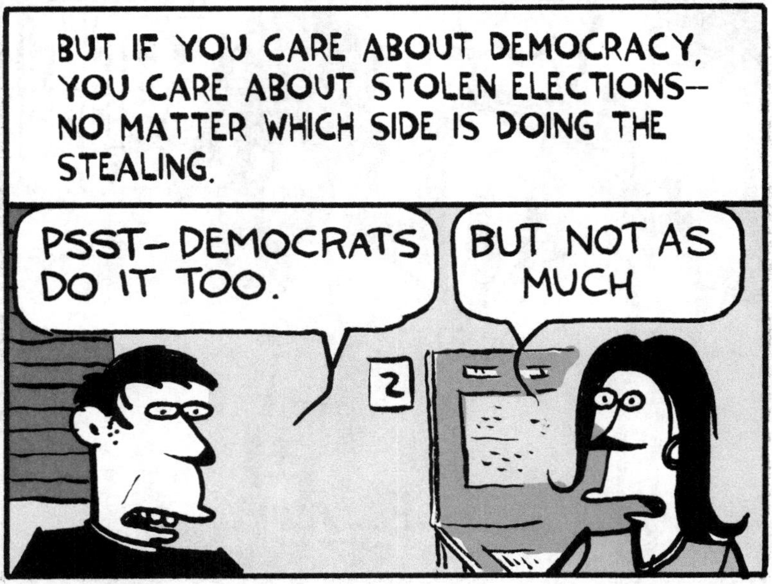
BUT IF YOU CARE ABOUT DEMOCRACY, YOU CARE ABOUT STOLEN ELECTIONS-- NO MATTER WHICH SIDE IS DOING THE STEALING.
PSST– DEMOCRATS DO IT TOO.
BUT NOT AS MUCH
2

ELECTION THIEVES MAINLY RELY ON 9 CLASSIC METHODS:

Purging.
Caging.
Spoiling.
Ejecting.

Blocking.
Rejecting.
Prestidigitizing.
Tossing.
Stuffing.

ON THE SURFACE, **PURGING** LOOKS PERFECTLY LEGIT.

CONVICTED FELONS CAN'T VOTE. NOR CAN ILLEGAL IMMIGRANTS. SO WE COMPARE LISTS OF REGISTERED VOTERS WITH LISTS OF FELONS AND KNOWN NON-CITIZENS, AND KICK OFF THE MATCHES.

WE USE COMPUTERS. TO PREVENT ERRORS.

IT'S SO... SCIENTIFIC.

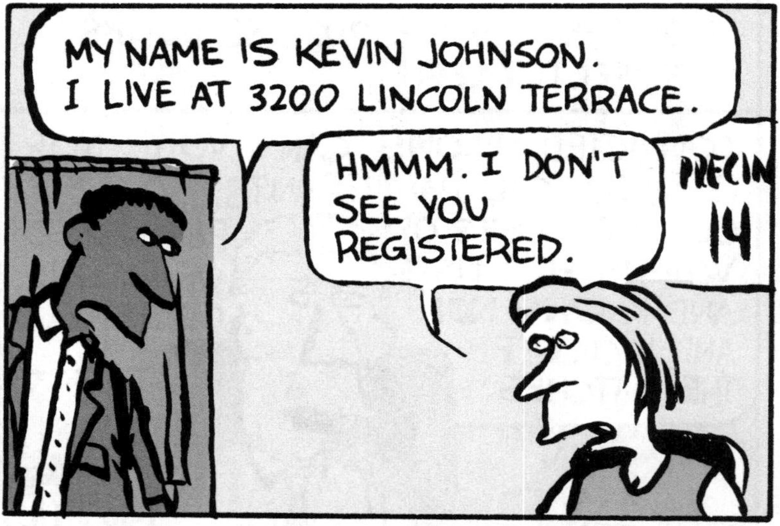
MY NAME IS KEVIN JOHNSON.
I LIVE AT 3200 LINCOLN TERRACE.
HMMM. I DON'T SEE YOU REGISTERED.
PRECIN
14

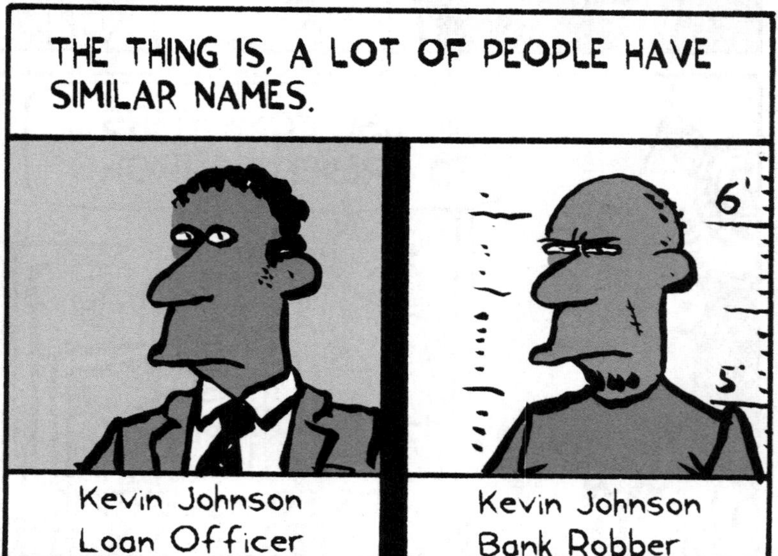
THE THING IS, A LOT OF PEOPLE HAVE SIMILAR NAMES.
6'
5'
Kevin Johnson
Loan Officer
Kevin Johnson
Bank Robber

AND, IN THE U.S., BECAUSE MORE ARE POOR AND FEW CAN AFFORD A DEFENSE, CONVICTED FELONS TEND TO BE BLACK.

Blacks amount to **13%** of U.S. population

but **39%** of prisoners

SINCE PEOPLE OF SIMILAR ETHNIC BACKGROUND TEND TO HAVE SIMILAR NAMES, PURGING A LIST OF BLACK FELONS, BASED ON NAME MATCH ALONE, HAS THE EFFECT OF PURGING LAW-ABIDING BLACKS.

LAW-ABIDING CITIZENS LOSE THEIR FRANCHISE SIMPLY BECAUSE THEIR NAMES RESEMBLE THOSE OF CRIMINALS THEY'VE NEVER MET.

BLACKS VOTE OVERWHELMINGLY DEMOCRATIC. (JOHN KERRY GOT 88% OF THE BLACK VOTE IN 2004, OBAMA GOT 96% IN 2008.) NATURALLY, REPUBLICAN OFFICIALS LOVE VOTER PURGES.

SAME GAME WITH THE "ILLEGAL IMMIGRANTS." IN STATES LIKE FLORIDA, LATINOS TEND TO VOTE DEMOCRATIC. AND LATINO NAMES TEND TO FIGURE PROMINENTLY ON LISTS OF UNDOCUMENTED WORKERS.

IN JUNE 2012, FOR EXAMPLE, THE DEPARTMENT OF JUSTICE ANNOUNCED PLANS TO FLORIDA'S SECRETARY OF STATE, A REPUBLICAN, FOR PURGING NATURALIZED CITIZENS.

AMONG THE VICTIMS: AT LEAST ONE DECORATED WAR VETERAN.

14

LIKE PURGING, **CAGING** IS A DIRTY TRICK DISGUISED BY A THIN VENEER OF LEGALITY. CAGERS MAIL LETTERS TO THE ADDRESSES ON RECORD FOR REGISTERED VOTERS, MARKED "DO NOT FORWARD."

SEEMS LOGICAL.

WE DON'T WANT FRAUDULENT VOTERS, RIGHT?

BUT IT'S OFTEN ILLEGAL. AND IT'S AN IMMORAL ASSAULT ON COMMON DECENCY.

CAGERS KNOW THAT THERE ARE MORE DATA ERRORS ON LISTS OF MINORITY VOTERS, WHO TEND TO VOTE DEMOCRATIC. AND THAT POOR PEOPLE MOVE A LOT (AND TEND TO VOTE DEMOCRATIC). AND COLLEGE STUDENTS AWAY AT COLLEGE. WHO TEND TO VOTE... YOU GOT IT.

16

REMEMBER THOSE HANGING CHADS?

FL(
21

THOSE ARE ONE EXAMPLE OF **SPOILED VOTES**—WHICH ARE SCREWED UP BY STUPIDITY OR BY CONFUSING VOTING INSTRUCTIONS, OR BOTH.

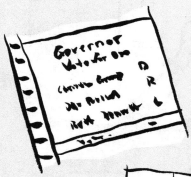

Undervotes:
Leaving a
Ballot Blank

Overvotes:
Casting more
than the
Permitted
Number of
Votes per Office

Physical Damage
to the Vote,
especially those
Counted by Machine

SOME SPOILED VOTES ARE HARD TO FIGURE OUT.

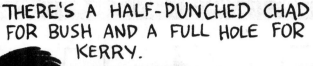
THERE'S A HALF-PUNCHED CHAD FOR BUSH AND A FULL HOLE FOR KERRY.

HERE'S A HALF-PUNCHED CHAD. LOOKS LIKE THE VOTER SIMPLY FAILED TO PUSH THE STYLUS ALL THE   WAY.

BUT NOT ALL.

THE FLORIDA SUPREME COURT ORDERED VOTE COUNTERS TO COUNT UNDERVOTES IN THE BUSH V. GORE RECOUNT IF THE "CLEAR INTENT OF THE VOTER" COULD BE DETERMINED.

EVEN THOUGH A CHAD WASN'T PUNCHED OUT COMPLETELY, OFFICIALS ASKED, WAS IT OBVIOUS THAT THE VOTER HAD TRIED TO?

DITTO FOR THE OVERVOTES. IF THE VOTER BOTH PUNCHED OUT THE HOLE INDICATING A VOTE FOR AL GORE AND WROTE HIS NAME ON THE CARD, SHE OBVIOUSLY INTENDED TO VOTE FOR GORE AND THAT VOTE SHOULD COUNT.

THERE ARE A LOT OF SPOILED VOTES. IN A TYPICAL U.S. PRESIDENTIAL ELECTION, 2 MILLION VOTES ARE COUNTED AS SPOILED AND TOSSED IN THE GARBAGE.

NOT ALL SPOILAGE IS EQUAL. THE U.S. CIVIL RIGHTS COMMISSION DISCOVERED THAT 54% OF SPOILED 2000 BALLOTS WERE CAST BY AFRICAN-AMERICANS. NATIONALLY, ABOUT 1 MILLION BLACK VOTES VANISHED INTO THE SPOILED PILE.

13% of the general population

54% of "spoiled" and disposed of ballots

ABOUT 90% OF THOSE THROWN AWAY, SPOILED VOTES, ARE FOR DEMOCRATS. OR WOULD BE.

HAD THE UNDERVOTES AND OVERVOTES FOR BOTH BUSH AND GORE BEEN COUNTED IN 2000, AL GORE WOULD HAVE BEEN DECLARED THE WINNER OF THE STATE OF FLORIDA, AND THUS BECOME PRESIDENT.

WOULD PRESIDENT GORE HAVE GONE TO WAR AGAINST AFGHANISTAN AFTER 9/11?

MAYBE.

WOULD HE HAVE GONE TO WAR AGAINST IRAQ?

PROBABLY NOT.

MILLIONS OF PEOPLE MIGHT STILL BE ALIVE— IF THE 2000 ELECTION HADN'T BEEN STOLEN.

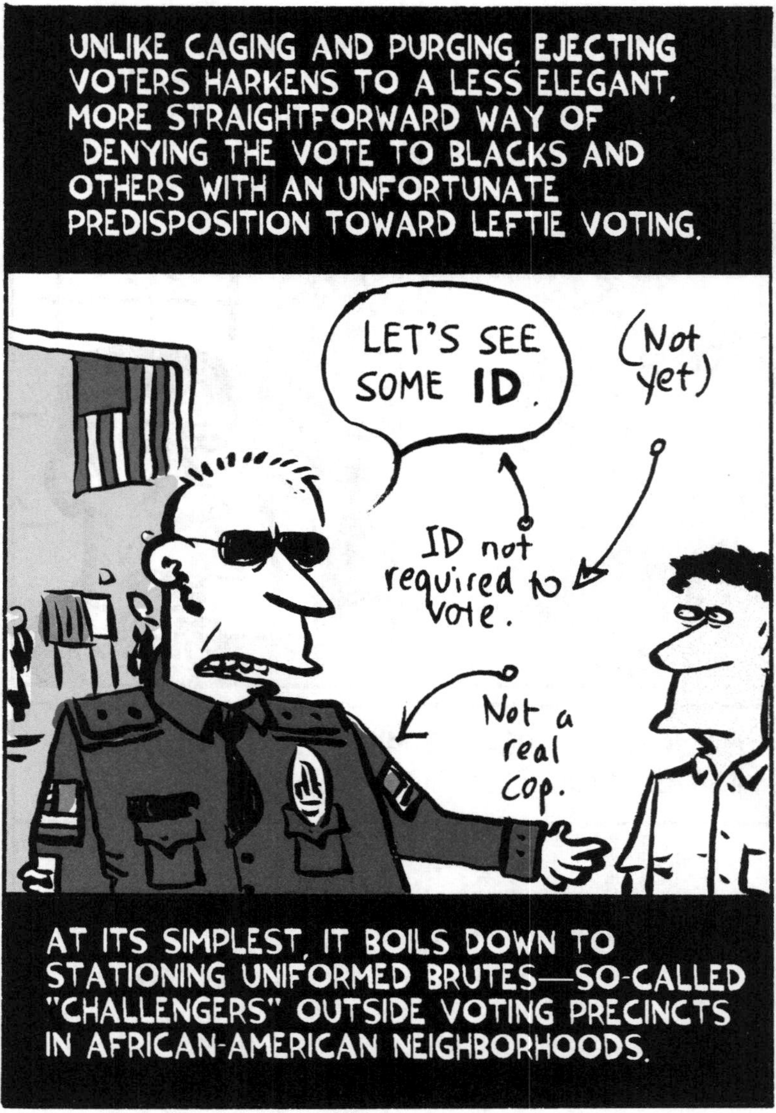
UNLIKE CAGING AND PURGING, EJECTING VOTERS HARKENS TO A LESS ELEGANT, MORE STRAIGHTFORWARD WAY OF DENYING THE VOTE TO BLACKS AND OTHERS WITH AN UNFORTUNATE PREDISPOSITION TOWARD LEFTIE VOTING.
LET'S SEE SOME **ID**.
(Not yet)
ID not required to vote.
Not a real cop.
AT ITS SIMPLEST, IT BOILS DOWN TO STATIONING UNIFORMED BRUTES—SO-CALLED "CHALLENGERS" OUTSIDE VOTING PRECINCTS IN AFRICAN-AMERICAN NEIGHBORHOODS.

STUFFING NEGATES LEGIT BALLOTS. CAGING AND PURGING GETS RID OF REAL VOTES ENTIRELY BY REMOVING LEGALLY REGISTERED VOTERS FROM THE ROLLS.

A GOP FUNCTIONARY GETS A WOULD-BE VOTER'S VOTE TOSSED—BUT SHE IS NEVER NOTIFIED OF HER DISENFRANCHISEMENT OR, FOR THAT MATTER, URGED TO CONFIRM HER REGISTRATION.

COMPANIES LIKE ES&S AND DIEBOLD,
BOTH FOUNDED BY REPUBLICAN ACTIVISTS,
SELL AND INSTALL ELECTRONIC VOTING
MACHINES THAT HAVE PROVEN TO BE
PERFECT TOOLS FOR PRESTIDIGITIZING
VOTE COUNTS.

"I am committed to helping Ohio deliver
its electoral votes to the president [Bush]
next year."
—Walden O'Dell
CEO of Diebold Inc, 2003

BECAUSE THERE IS NO PAPER RECORD, NO OPEN SOURCE CODE—IN SHORT, NO TRANSPARENCY WHATSOEVER—THESE COMPUTERIZED BALLOT MONSTERS ARE TAILOR-MADE FOR MANIPULATING VOTE COUNTS.

IN ONE ELECTION IN TEXAS, FOR EXAMPLE, 3 REPUBLICANS EACH WON WITH EXACTLY 18,181 VOTES. (IN THOSE RACES, THE "LOSING" DEMOCRATS INSISTED UPON A RECOUNT—AND WON.)

COMAL COUNTY TX

State Senator	Jeff Wentworth	18,181	R
State Rep.	Carter Casteel	18,181	R
Judge	Danny Scheel	18,181	R

THE ECONOMY SUCKS. BUT SOME SECTORS ARE DOING GREAT.

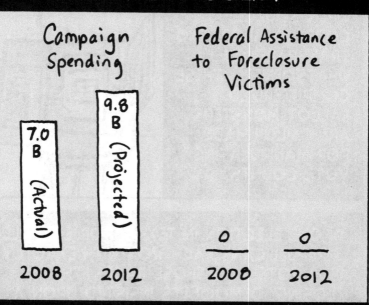

Campaign Spending

7.0 B (Actual)	9.8 B (Projected)
2008	2012

Federal Assistance to Foreclosure Victims

0	0
2008	2012

THIS STIMULUS COMES COURTESY OF THE "CITIZENS UNITED" RULING, WHICH ELIMINATED LIMITS ON THE AMOUNTS THAT SHADOWY CORPORATIONS (AND ANYONE ELSE) CAN CONTRIBUTE TO CAMPAIGNS.

IN 2012, 48% OF CONTRIBUTIONS WILL COME FROM PACS, NATIONAL POLITICAL PARTY COMMITTEES, AND SUPERPACS.

GET THE MONEY OUT OF POLITICS

OCCUPY

THAT'S THE DEMAND OF THOSE WHO HATE THAT DEMOCRACY HAS BEEN HIJACKED.

BUT WHY IS ALL THAT MONEY IN POLITICS IN THE FIRST PLACE? HOW DO CAMPAIGNS SPEND IT?

"FedEx shipments, staff salaries, flights from Washington, D.C., to Des Moines to Las Vegas and back again — it all adds up.
—Tom Curry
  MSNBC, 2007

AND TV ADS.
LOTS AND LOTS OF TV ADS.

AT LEAST THAT'S WHAT THE MEDIA TELLS US.

"In politics there is certainly no linear relationship between amount of money and degree of success. Just ask the well-heeled Republican losers of presidential primaries past — former Texas Governor John Connally, former Texas Senator Phil Gramm, and former mayor and front-runner Rudolph Giuliani...Big money without the right message can become a penny waiting for change.

—Bob Shrum, Democratic Senior Advisor

THEY SAY THAT MONEY DOESN'T MAKE A HUGE DIFFERENCE. THAT, IN THE END, GOOD IDEAS ARE WHAT'S REALLY DETERMINATIVE.

BUT THAT'S NOT HOW IT REALLY IS.

Charismatic

Brilliant
Speaker

Inspiring

↪

Didn't
stand a
chance
without
wealthy
backers ←

SURE, TV ADS ARE EXPENSIVE. BUT A BIG SHARE OF THAT LOOT—ESPECIALLY ANONYMOUS PAC AND SUPERPAC CASH—GOES INTO MAINTAINING DATABASES.

DATABASES OF VOTERS. OF FELONS. OF IMMIGRANTS.

OF LIKELY DEMOCRATIC VOTERS.

541-23-1213   Jackson,
                 Criminal
                 Possessio

417-00-9811   Jackson
                 Suspecte
                 Undocm

TO BE TARGETED. ELIMINATED.

TO HAVE THEIR VOTES DISAPPEAR.

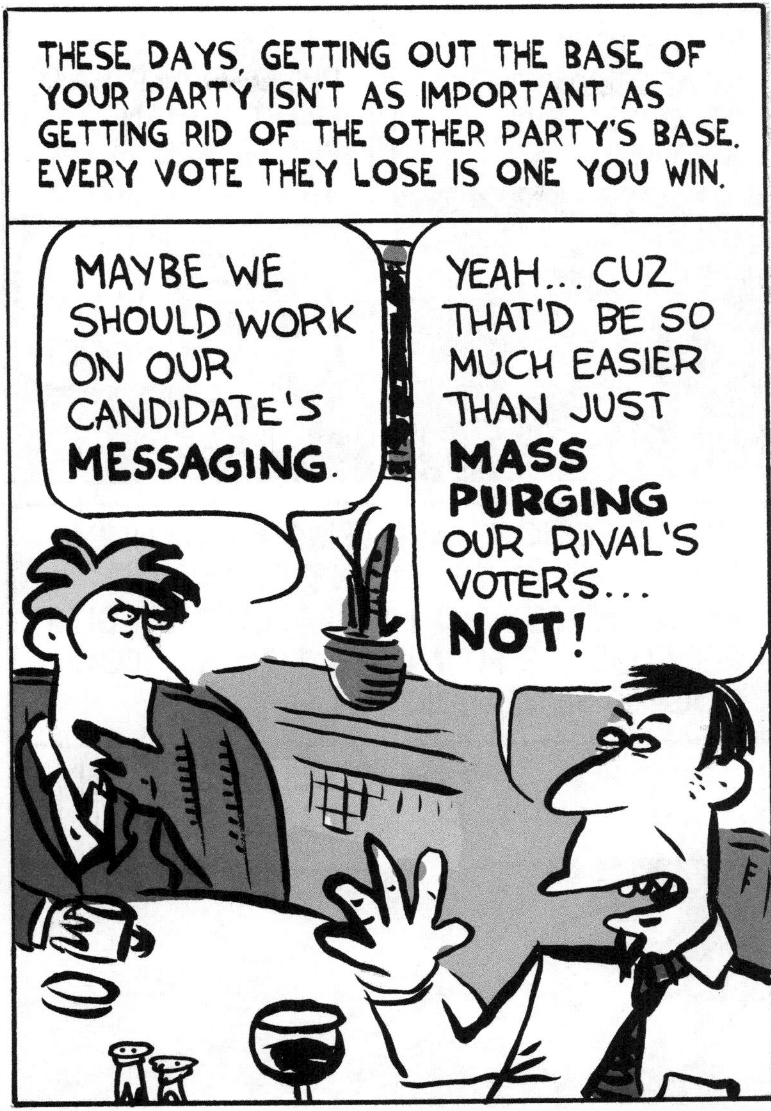
THESE DAYS, GETTING OUT THE BASE OF YOUR PARTY ISN'T AS IMPORTANT AS GETTING RID OF THE OTHER PARTY'S BASE. EVERY VOTE THEY LOSE IS ONE YOU WIN.
MAYBE WE SHOULD WORK ON OUR CANDIDATE'S **MESSAGING**.
YEAH... CUZ THAT'D BE SO MUCH EASIER THAN JUST **MASS PURGING** OUR RIVAL'S VOTERS... **NOT!**

WHO'S BEHIND THESE SCARCELY REPORTED EVIL SHENANIGANS?

AS THE PHILOSOPHER SAID, MOST HUMAN BEINGS ARE BASICALLY GOOD.

I BLAME SOCIETY.

OUR ELECTIONS ARE BEING STOLEN BY THE OTHER ONES: A TINY CABAL OF BILLIONAIRES WHO HIRE BALLOT BANDITS BECAUSE, AS MTV USED TO SAY, TOO MUCH IS NEVER ENOUGH.

SOMEWHERE SOMEONE IS GETTING A PENNY THAT OUGHT TO BE **MINE**.

HAROLD SIMMONS OF TEXAS, WORTH NEARLY $10 BILLION, IS THE ICE MAN. THE #1 GOP DONOR WILL SHELL OUT OVER $50 MILLION IN 2012 TO SUPERPACS. (HE EARNED HIS NICKNAME—FROM HIS FRIENDS—FOR HIS BRUTAL TACTICS AS A CORPORATE RAIDER.)

THE ICE MAN'S MOTIVES ARE SIMPLE. HE'S IN THE TOXIC WASTE DISPOSAL BUSINESS. HE WANTS TO ELECT PLANET-HATING REPUBLICANS TO GET RID OF ENVIRONMENTAL REGULATIONS THAT REDUCE HIS PROFITS.

MEET THE VULTURE: PAUL SINGER, #1 DONOR TO THE MITT ROMNEY SUPERPAC AND THE NEW YORK STATE REPUBLICAN PARTY. THE VULTURE—LIKE THE ICE MAN, NAMED BY HIS CLOSEST PALS—ALSO HATES ENVIRONMENTAL RULES BECAUSE THEY CRIMPED HIS ASBESTOS BUSINESS.

37

THE VULTURE'S MAIN BUSINESS, HOWEVER, IS SNATCHING UP THIRD-WORLD DEBT FOR PENNIES ON THE DOLLAR, THEN FORECLOSING ON THE COLLATERAL FROM DESPERATELY POOR COUNTRIES.

THE VULTURE EVEN TRIED TO SEIZE THE CONGOLESE EMBASSY IN D.C., BUT THE OBAMA ADMINISTRATION STOPPED HIM. A 100% BOUGHT-AND-PAID-FOR WHITE HOUSE WOULDN'T HAVE INTERFERED.

THE KOCH BROTHERS, CHARLIE AND DAVID, EACH WORTH $20 BILLION, ARE CLASSIC OIL MEN FROM TEXAS. IT HARDLY NEEDS EXPLAINING WHY THEY WANT POLITICAL INFLUENCE.

THESE DAYS THEY WANT TO GREENLIGHT THE KEYSTONE XL PIPELINE, WHICH WOULD BRING BUSINESS TO ONE OF THEIR TEXAS REFINERIES.

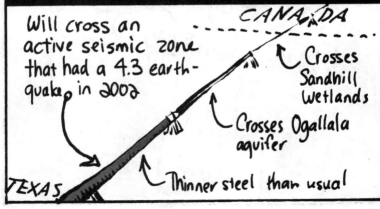

BILLIONAIRES BUY DEMOCRATS TOO. DURING THE 1990S THE RIADY FAMILY OF INDONESIA CORRUPTED PRESIDENT CLINTON AND HIS WIFE HILLARY WITH INDIRECT DONATIONS TO CLINTON CRONIES.

40

WHILE THE CLINTONS' PALS GOT GREASED, THE RIADYS CONVINCED THE PRESIDENT TO COZY UP TO INDONESIAN DICTATOR SUHARTO AND TO QUASH REPORTS ABOUT OPPRESSION IN EAST TIMOR.

Jailed, killed and banned dissidents

Estimated family wealth: $15 billion (1999)

THE CLINTONS CAME CHEAP. THE RIADYS ONLY SHELLED OUT A MILLION BUCKS OF CASH FOR A BILLION WORTH OF INFLUENCE.

$1 million

buys you a studio apt. in Manhattan

or a President

TEXAS OIL MEN **ANDREW AND SAM WYLY** BACKED GEORGE W. BUSH'S DIRTY 2000 PRIMARY WIN OVER JOHN MCCAIN. MCCAIN RETALIATED WITH HIS CAMPAIGN FINANCE REFORM LAW. BUSH THEN APPOINTED JUSTICE JOHN ROBERTS TO GUT IT.

M c CAIN HAS A BASTARD DAUGHTER. HE'S GAY. HE CHEATED ON HIS DRUG-ADDICT WIFE.

THE S.E.C. LATER ACCUSED THE WYLYS OF EARNING THEIR SEED MONEY—$550 MILLION—THROUGH FRAUD.

OBAMA HAS HIS OWN BILLIONAIRE PATRON: PENNY PRITZKER. WORTH $1.7 BILLION, PRITZKER IS A PREDATORY BANKSTER WHOSE EXPLOITATIVE SUBPRIME LENDING OPERATIONS AND RACIST REDLINING HURT COUNTLESS CHICAGOANS.

SHE WAS OBAMA'S NATIONAL FINANCE CHAIR AND A MEMBER OF THE PRESIDENT'S COUNCIL OF ECONOMIC ADVISORS. NOT BAD FOR A CONWOMAN.

She's on a Spending Spree!

Donated to Bush, to McCain, to Gore, to Hillary...

MAYBE YOU DON'T CARE WHAT THESE BILLIONAIRES AND THEIR HIRED BALLOT BANDITS ARE UP TO.

BUT THEY CARE. ODDS ARE, ANYTHING THEY'RE INTO IS BAD FOR YOU.

SO WE SHOULD STOP THEM.

44

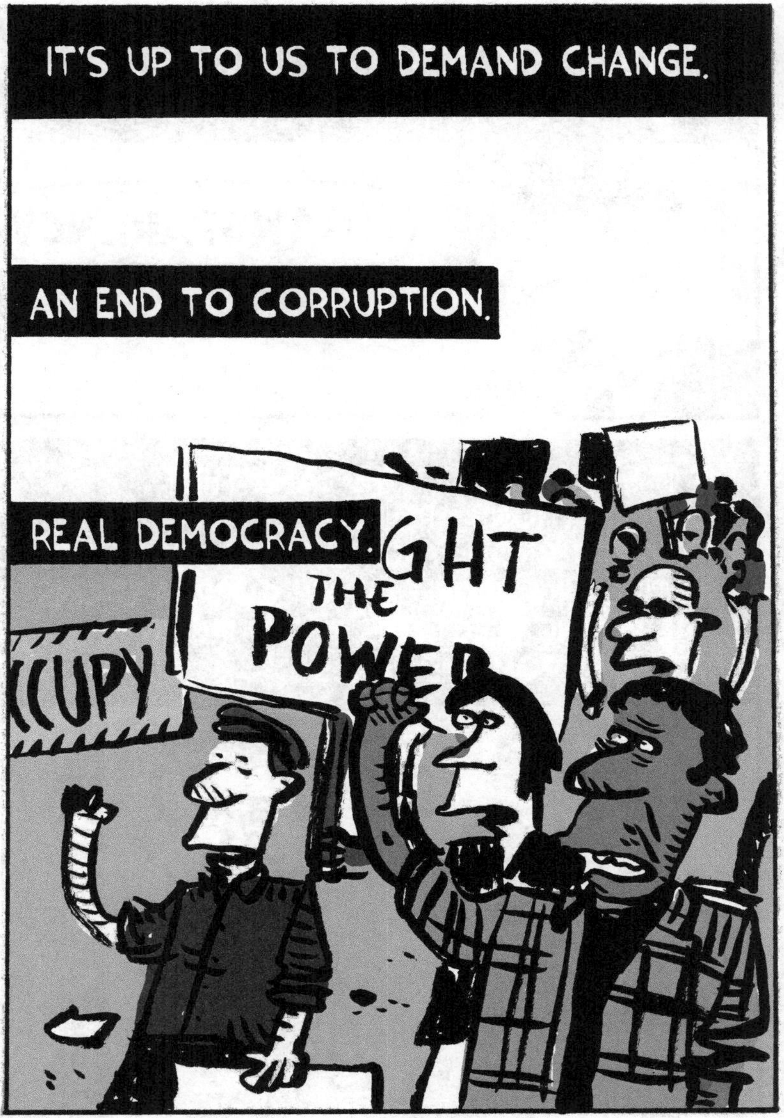
IT'S UP TO US TO DEMAND CHANGE.
AN END TO CORRUPTION.
REAL DEMOCRACY.
GHT THE POWER
CCUPY

START BY DEMANDING SOMETHING SO REASONABLE THAT THEY'LL FIND IT HARD TO REFUSE US: TRANSPARENCY.

IF IT'S THE LAW OF THE LAND THAT CORPORATIONS ARE PEOPLE, WE HAVE THE RIGHT TO KNOW WHICH CORPORATIONS ARE ACTING LIKE PEOPLE, WHICH CORPORATIONS ARE BUYING ELECTIONS AND PURGING VOTERS FROM THE ROLLS.

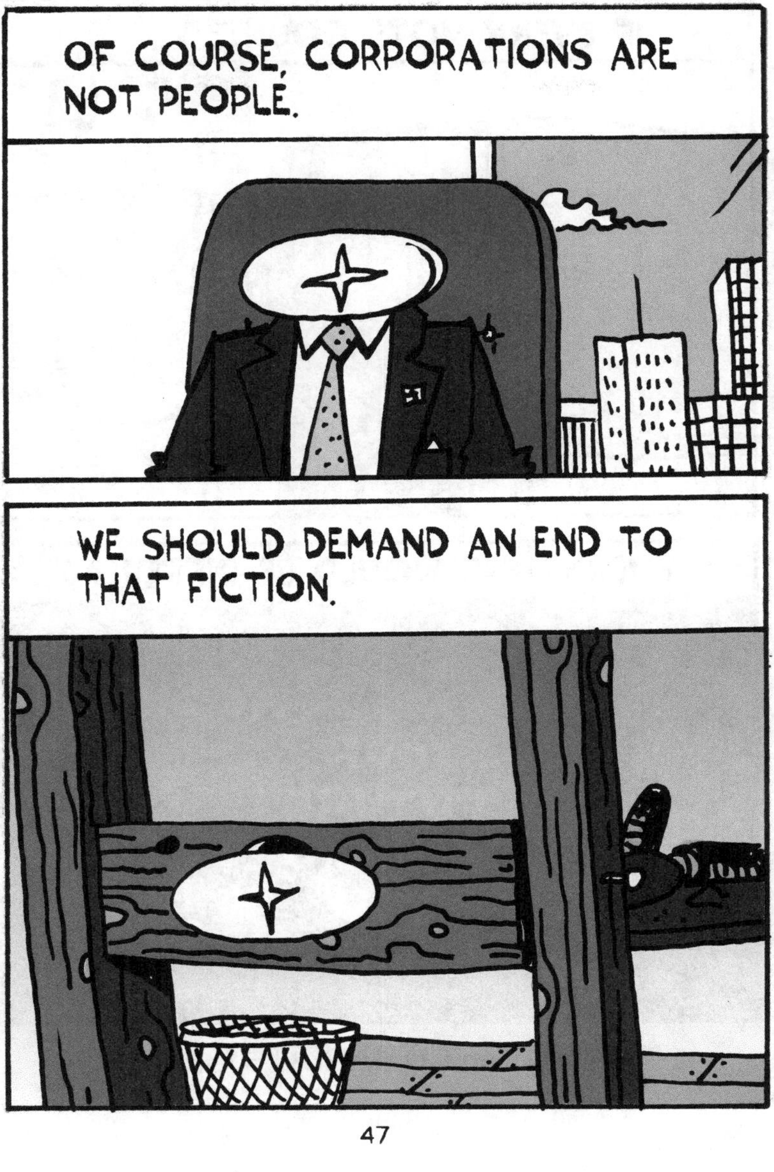
OF COURSE, CORPORATIONS ARE NOT PEOPLE.
WE SHOULD DEMAND AN END TO THAT FICTION.

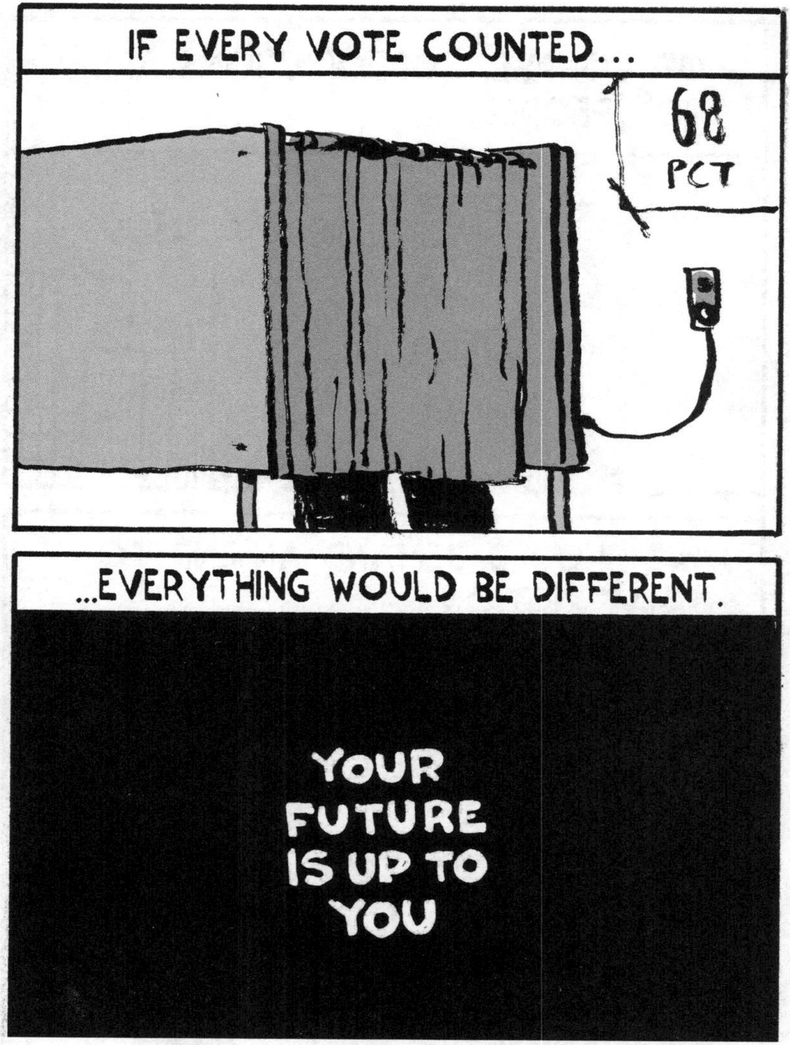
IF EVERY VOTE COUNTED...
68 PCT
...EVERYTHING WOULD BE DIFFERENT.
YOUR FUTURE IS UP TO YOU

WWW.BALLOTBANDITS.ORG

directed the Colorado governor's task force on voting. (When politicians want to avoid a problem, they organize a task force.) Hultin, an attorney of unquestioned integrity, knows his stuff. The purge in Colorado made him ill.

While the task force was busy with its task (assigned to report one month *after* the election), the secretary of state was busy with the voter-roll scrub brush. And Hultin's task force was kept in the dark.

Hultin had other matters to deal with. A federal judge ruled that Colorado's electronic voting machines were "abysmal," error-ridden, and a hacker's dream. In other words, just what Rove had ordered. In 2009, Colorado promised the judge they'd move back to paper ballots— right *after* the 2012 election.

And I also discovered this: just weeks before the 2004 election, Secretary of State Davidson pulled a Kate Harris, removing several thousand voters from the state's rolls, folks she tagged as "felons."

What makes this particularly noteworthy is that, unlike Florida, Colorado *does not bar ex-cons from voting.*

Indeed, federal law bars purges within ninety days of a presidential election to allow voters time to challenge their loss of civil rights. But so no victim could say, *WTF???*, she pulled this one off just days before the election.

To exempt her action from the federal rule, Secretary Davidson declared an "emergency." However, the only "emergency" in Colorado seemed to be dead-even poll numbers.

Why the sudden urge to purge? Davidson's chief of voting-law enforcement was Drew Durham, who previously worked for the attorney general of Texas. This is what the former spokeswoman for the Lone Star State's attorney general says of Mr. Durham: He is "unfit for public office . . . a man with a history of racism and ideological zealotry."

In other words, perfect for the job.

■ ■ ■

Clearly, Donetta had replaced Katherine as queen of voter-roll cleaning, scrubbing the Colorado registries whiter than white. In honor of her work, President George Bush named her chairwoman of the Election Assistance Commission, where she could direct the scrub-a-dub of the entire nation's voter rolls and election machinery.

As she'd already flown to Washington to take up her post as the nation's Purge'n General, I hopped a plane to the Capitol. There, Donetta took the opportunity to lock me out of her new office.

Today, under President Obama, the Election Assistance Commission's door is open . . . but no one's home. There is not one single election commissioner—the Republicans in the US Senate will not confirm any appointment from either party, and have nearly eliminated the commission's funding. One cost-saving measure: the Election Commission will no longer issue the report with the purge statistics that tipped me off to the biggest attack on civil rights since the Klan beat Martin Luther King's marchers on the way from Montgomery to Selma.

But while she was there, Donetta and secretaries of state across the USA did their job. From 2004 through 2006, computers were unleashed on the voter rolls and, like Pac-Men gone wild, ate ten million names.

And this year, the pace has quickened.

Has the press noticed? Oh, yes: America's media has decided that not enough voters have been barred. The *Wall Street Journal* has been running John Fund's phantasmagorical allegations of voter fraud, the legions of illegal voters on the rolls.

■ ■ ■

Despite the urban myth of the Election Night of the Living Voter, the number of dead people voting (by live folk taking their names) is virtually nonexistent. In Michigan, Dr. Minnite investigated the twenty-seven cases of dead voters in Detroit cited by "expert" Thor Hearne whom the Republican congressmen have paraded through hearings. These were all absentee voters (*very* absent). However, as in every single verified case of zombie voters investigated, the dead licked their own stamps: all were voters who passed away after mailing in their ballots.

In December 2006, the Election Commission issued the vote-fraud hysteria magna carta, with the pulp fiction title *Election Crimes*. It talked of reviewing "more than forty thousand cases" of voter fraud and intimidation, including "absentee ballot fraud, voter registration fraud, multiple voting, felons voting, vote buying."

Of course, the report didn't actually say there were forty thousand fraudulent voters or any votes for sale on eBay, nor gazillions of serial "multiple" voters running wild from polling booth to polling both filling out stacks of ballots.

But it sure did give that impression.

The two authors of *Crimes* are Job Serebrov and Tova Wang. Dr. Wang is one of the most respected names in the field of voting integrity, so that she would write *Election Crimes* was astonishing.

And it was a lie. She didn't write it. In 2008, I found Dr. Wang in Washington.

I showed her *Crimes;* she said it wasn't hers. Then I showed her a copy of a report that had come my way, called *Voting Fraud and Voter Intimidation*. It's the report she actually wrote with her politically conservative partner Serebrov.

It was not the potboiler that had been issued in her name. Not close.

Then Dr. Wang told me a story that made me look out the window at the US Capitol just to make sure I wasn't in North Korea.[9] The real report concluded,

"Narrow voter identification requirements cause perfectly eligible voters, disproportionately minorities or the elderly, disproportionately Democratic, to lose their vote."

Ten million voters would lose their vote in the hysterical, phony crusade to block that evil fraudulent voter. And how many of these evildoers are there? That's when she noted,

"I would say that your chances of being hit by lightning are far greater than you finding a non-citizen who's voted in an election."

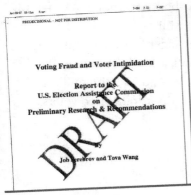

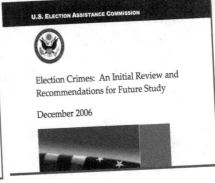

---

9   I encourage you to read my entire discussion with Dr. Wang and meet her in the film *Billionaires & Ballot Bandits*, which you can download at www. BallotBandits.com.

She and her expert colleague concluded that the real voting problem in America was *"intimidation"* and *"suppression"* of the vote by the likes of Colorado Secretary of State Donetta Davidson.

But then something happened. Dr. Wang's boss, *Donetta Davidson,* and other Bush appointees prevented her from speaking to the federal commissioners. They rewrote her report, standing her findings on their head, named it *Election Crimes,* with her name and stature still attached, and ordered her to shut-the-@#$%-up or they'd fire her. And then they went further: the Bush administration would sue her, bankrupt her, destroy her, if she spoke out, even if she quit.

She spoke out, lost her job, then beat the government's legal attack with the help of a pro-bono attorney and some outraged congressmen (there are still a couple of those).

But the damage was done: the federal government had officially endorsed purges, ID laws, and all the tools of the new Jim Crow ballot-box blockade. And, in 2012, millions more will join five million already disenfranchised voters.

20.

The Ex-Con Con-Job

And by the way, ex-cons *can* vote. In all but six states, almost anyone convicted of a felony crime who's served their sentence can vote.

In only *three* states (Kentucky, Virgina, and Florida) is there a near-total ban on voting by ex-cons. Another seven Ku Klux Klan states restrict ex-cons' civil rights. (That's not a cheap slur: the felon-voter ban was drafted and passed by Klansmen-controlled legislatures during Reconstruction.)

The ex-con vote is potentially bigger and more significant to the outcome of the 2012 presidential race than the Hispanic vote.

The number of ex-cons in the US is 19.8 million—and growing fast. One in eleven Americans has a felony conviction. More than sixteen *million* of them are eligible to vote—and according to Professor Jeff Manza, about 89 percent vote Democratic or would if they could.

So how come no one's talking about it? How come the Obama campaign doesn't say, *"We may be behind in the white male demographic, but we've more than made up for it among ex-felons"?*

Again, I'm not talking about ex-cons not allowed to vote in Ku Klux Florida, nor about the seven million Americans serving time. I'm talking about the vast majority of ex-cons who have served their sentences and now *have the right to vote, don't know it, and don't act on it.*

Why aren't these citizens registered?

Partly, it's because no one in power will defend the rights of the least powerful people in America. (Actually, that's not true: the armed wing of the GOP has worked hard to protect the rights of ex-cons and future cons to get a *gun.*)

The only presidential candidates in the last half-century to stand up during a campaign for the right of ex-felons to vote were Senators Hillary Clinton and, courageously, Rick Santorum. (That is why they ripped the sleeves off his sweater.) Santorum, in a televised debate in the Deep South, no less, brought up the topic out of the blue:

"I would ask Governor Romney: Do you believe people who have—who were felons, who've served their time, who've exhausted their parole and probation, should they be given the right to vote?"

Romney was befuddled and lost. There was silence

except for the loud, nervous tick-tock, tick-tock coming from Romney's head.

"We have plenty of time," Romney spluttered. "I'll get there."

He never quite arrived, but, weaving along the way, he came down on the side of guns-not-votes for felons. Santorum then informed a surprised Romney, former Governor of Massachusetts, that his own state never took away the right to vote from ex-cons. Indeed, Massachusetts even allows some convicts to vote from prison. Many voted for Romney (go figure).

Back to my question: How is it that maybe ten million ex-cons, eligible to vote, don't?

To a great extent, it's because, like the ex-Governor of Massachusetts, they don't know the law.

And politicians want to keep it that way. So they lie. The myth that ex-cons can't vote is so strong (and politically useful) that it's easy to convince these citizens, and even some elections officials, to bar felons from voting. Colorado wasn't alone in conducting massive ex-con purges without a legal justification.

And sometimes, the con by the politicians is deliberate. In 2000, when I discovered that Katherine Harris had targeted ninety-one thousand legal voters as felons barred from voting, I obtained from a nervous insider in Harris's office the info that thousands on the list were ex-cons who *had* the right to vote. Furthermore, there were another *forty thousand* ex-cons in Florida *with* the right to vote—but who were barred anyway.

Huh? These forty thousand ex-cons had *moved to* Florida. As most states don't take away your right to vote, you can't suddenly lose that right merely by driving over the Florida state line. That violates federal law. The law in question is called the Constitution. The "comity" clause in that document prevents one state from ignoring the court judgments of another.

Staring at the computer screen for several hours, coming back to it and staring again, this is what I discovered: On September 18, 2000, Governor Jeb Bush's office ordered every county clerk in the state to block or purge the registration of citizens with convictions *in other states*. The order came down after one clerk refused to "break the law" by denying someone their vote without a specific order from the governor. So, the governor's office literally *ordered* the clerks to commit a federal crime, to violate the Voting Rights Act and Constitution.

When I blew the whistle, it was already too late. The felon purge had allowed George Bush to claim victory on the basis of a rigged vote.

While US newspapers didn't give a damn, the US Civil Rights Commission was wowed by the info and demanded the state of Florida open its files to investigators. The commission backed my finding that thousands of black voters

FL THOMPSON, DOYLE TRAVIS

FL ALDRIDGE, LOYAL EDDIE

OH COOPER, THOMAS

FL RAMOS, MIGUEL

HALL, ARTHUR LEE

without any record were purged as "felons." Harder to find was evidence that ex-cons from other states had been purged illegally and deliberately.

So I called Katherine Harris's office and told a clerk, "Katherine said she got a letter from Governor Bush's office telling her to order the purge of ex-cons from other states. She'd like me to see it. Could you send me a copy?"

And ten minutes later, in my fax machine, there it was—the smoking gun still smoking:

STATE OF FLORIDA

JEB BUSH, GOVERNOR, CHAIRMAN
KATHERINE HARRIS, SECRETARY OF STATE
ROBERT A. BUTTERWORTH, ATTORNEY GENERAL
ROBERT F. MILLIGAN, COMPTROLLER

BILL NELSON, TREASURER
TOM GALLAGHER, COMMISSIONER OF EDUCATION
BOB CRAWFORD, COMMISSIONER OF AGRICULTURE
MRS. JANET H. KELLS, COORDINATOR

PHONE: 850/488-29

OFFICE OF EXECUTIVE CLEMENCY
2601 BLAIRSTONE ROAD
BUILDING C, ROOM 229
TALLAHASSEE, FLORIDA 32399-2450

September 18, 2000

Mr. Ed Kast, Assistant ~~~~ctor
Division of Elections
Department of State
The Capitol, Room 1801
Tallahassee, Fl. 32399-0250

Dear Mr. Kast:

Pursuant to your letter of August 10 and ou~~~ ~~~ver ~~~ ~~ this date, this is to advise you that a certificate of restoration of civil rights, relief o~~~ ~~~~~s, or pardon order issued by a court, agency, clemency board, or governor of anoth~~~ ~~~~ ~~~~ognized by the Office of Executive Clemency as restoring civil rights in the St~~~ ~~~~ ~~~hese individuals do not need to make application with the Office of Executive Clemen~~~~.

Any individual whose civil rights were restored automatically by statute in the state of conviction, and does not have a written certificate or order, would be required to make application for restoration of civil rights in the State of Florida.

So, do I believe Katherine Harris should be allowed to vote? Or Jeb Bush? After all, they committed a felony crime, violating both the Civil Rights Act and the Voting Rights Act. I say, let them vote—but only after they've served their time.

Oh, yeah: that's not a minor point. No state stops *criminals* from voting, only cons, people *convicted* of crimes, crimes like "doing a little blow," as Barack "Little Blow" Obama put it. Crimes like possessing pot, like Bill "But

I Didn't Inhale" Clinton, or "*lots* of blow," as George W. "That Was a Long Time Ago" Bush might say.

One in four adult African Americans have convictions for felony crimes, not because they necessarily commit more crimes but because they do necessarily get convicted more frequently.

I found an ex-con who'd moved to Florida and informed him that he could vote. That came as quite a surprise to the Reverend Thomas Johnson, who had sued the state to overturn the ban on his voting, not realizing he already possessed the right. (It took his lawyers from the ACLU by surprise as well. Like I told you, this is not an easy issue to understand.)

Reverend Johnson had sold crack in New York, went to prison, came out, found God, and went to work with ex-cons in Gainesville, Florida.

He told me, "We must bring people who've paid their price to society back into that society. Give them a stake in it." Well, that's fancy talk. In most of the world, since the fall of the Soviet Union, you don't become a noncitizen because of a prison term long ago served.

So, when, armed with the court order, Reverend Johnson went back to register at the Alachua County office which had turned him away, they were stunned to see the militant African American's voter form. The surprised clerk peered at the form and told him, "Well, if we'd known you were going to register as a *Republican*, we wouldn't have turned you down."

Why would a black man register for the party that tried to block his registration? Well, he could say that, after all, it was the Democratic Party that drafted all the Jim Crow laws, and the only two governors to actively work against the ban on ex-con voting were a Republican governor of Florida, Charlie Crist, and a governor of Texas, George W. Bush.

In fact, Obama owes his knife-edge victory in Florida in 2008 entirely to Crist's allowing a few thousand ex-cons the vote. The GOP punished Crist and threw his political career to the alligators. Florida GOP hacks re-banned "felon" voters. Sympathy for the ex-slave citizenry is gone.

A University of Minnesota study by Jeff Manza and Christopher Uggen confirmed that the presidency in 2000 was determined by the ex-con wipeout. They also calculated that seven Senate seats, and control of Congress, also went to the GOP via the ex-con con. In 2012, muscled up with their HAVA purge powers, GOP secretaries of state are preparing to take Congress again with the ex-con con, especially, I've discovered, in Ohio, Colorado, Arizona, Wisconsin, and, of course, the Sunblind State.

If Obama loses Florida this time, it will be wholly due to the tens of thousands of out-of-state ex-felons and in-state faux felons purged, blocked, or barred from the voter rolls.

(It's only fair, I suppose, for the Republicans to lynch by laptop: the laws were originally passed by Democratic legislatures using the catchy slogan, "End the Danger of Negro Dominance.")

Here's the Florida GOP at it again. Check out this post–Katherine Harris purge list:

```
4/13/42/BLA

Brown, Thomas J
7/22/55/BLA

Brown, Thomas John
1/13/72/WHI

rell, James H
/60/WHI
```

```
Brown, Thomas Jeffer
4/13/42/BLA/FLA co

Brown, Thomas Jerald
7/22/55/WHI/FL con

Brown, Thomas
1/13/72/BLA/SC con.
```

There's Thomas Brown, a black voter purged because a *white* man named Thomas Brown, with the same birthday, committed a felony. And then there's *another* Thomas Brown who has been purged because yet another Thomas Brown was convicted of a crime in South Carolina in violation of court orders and the Constitution. (South Carolina, like most states, does not take away your right to vote after you've served your time.)

This list marks the return of Jim Crow, though his business card now reads, James Crow, Systems Analyst, Database Management Services.

JOIN OUR ACTION LIST AT www.BallotBandits.org and get a free, gratis, no-cost, zero-down, zero-later digital copy of our other comic book on election theft. By Greg Palast and Bobby Kennedy, with Ted Rall, Lloyd Dangle, and the comic geniuses that brought you *Billionaires & Ballot Bandits*.

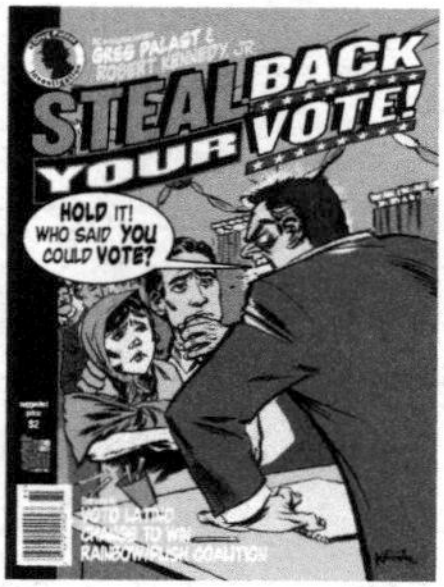
STEAL BACK YOUR VOTE!
HOLD IT! WHO SAID YOU COULD VOTE?

Sign up for updates on the election heists, info on actions to stop them, and the latest on the Vulture, the Ice Man, and the Rove-bots.

21.

Indians Spoiled Rotten

In 2004, I got a report that only one in ten voters in nine precincts in McKinley County, New Mexico—74.7 percent of them Navajo—voted without choosing a president. They drove miles across the Navajo reservation, walked into the voting booth, then said, "Nah, forget it," and didn't vote for president of the USA.

Or, at least that's the official story. That's what the tallies show.

Indeed, all over the Southwest, Native Americans by the tens of thousands are to this day seized with indecision when confronted with a choice in a voting booth. Coincidentally, Natives register more than seven-to-one Democratic. Coincidentally.

In the Taos Pueblo, "blank" nearly beat the Democratic candidate. That's what the machines said.

And when you have a precinct that combines Pueblo

Indians with poor Hispanics, just forget it: these voters just don't give a damn. For example, in a special precinct in dirt-poor Doña Ana County created to collect absentee ballots from soldiers overseas, not a single Native or Mexican American doughboy listed a choice for their commander-in-chief. *One hundred percent blank, not one voted for President of the United States.*

That's the official story. That's what the tallies show. Again.

White voters are more decisive. Here, the official story as told by the vote-tallying machines is quite different. In precincts in the suburban upper-income ring around Albuquerque (where voters use paper ballots, not machines), *101 percent of voters* chose a president. Most of these, including the ghosts who voted, are big for the GOP.

Call me crazy, but something seemed wrong here. So I reached New Mexico's Secretary of State

Becky Vigil-Giron on her cell while she was driving to the Capitol from Albuquerque. This was before her indictment (that business about corrupt contracts for voting machines). I asked her about the missing Hispanic and Native military votes. The secretary of state told me, "Well, a lot of *these people can't make up their minds*."

Okay, Madame Secretary, that answer works for US media bobbleheads, but the BBC thought I should actually go and meet some of these indecisive Indians.

So I went down to one of the Southwest's blank-ballot hot spots, the Laguna and Acoma Pueblos of New Mexico, home of what were, according to voting machines, some of the nation's most indecisive voters. In 2004, these Natives suffered eighteen times the national average of blank or spoiled ballots.

Though the secretary of state says "these people" simply can't make up their minds, they didn't seem indecisive to me. They held strong opinions. "The war is a sin," pueblo leader David Ballo told me—and so was voting for Bush the Sinner.

Maybe there's another explanation: maybe the machines failed to register their votes. Few Americans realize that in the 2008 presidential election, nearly a million and a half ballots were left uncounted because they were supposedly unreadable, blank, or just somehow lost in the machines.

How does a ballot get spoiled? Not by leaving it out of the fridge.

Remember the belly laughs the press got out of the "hanging chads" during the Florida vote count in 2000?

What's so funny? Every hanging chad is a vote that didn't get counted. And there were lots and lots of hung votes. We got our hands on a Florida voting machine with chads still in it. They're no bigger than Al Gore's teardrops. Check out my chad:

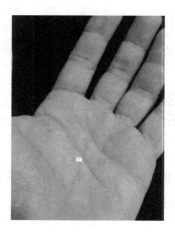

On punch-card ballots, you have to poke out a hole in the cardboard with a metal thing-y. Sometimes you poke the hole and a little piece of it just hangs there by a corner. You don't even see it.

In the old days, before the US Supreme Court became the Supreme Corp, the voter's intent determined if your ballot counted. If you punched a hole, even if the little bugger didn't fall out completely, it's damn certain whom you voted for, and the vote counted.

But not in Florida in 2000, nor in Ohio in 2004, nor in too many states today. In Florida, Secretary of State Katherine Harris ruled that if a hole was punched but the "chad" hadn't dropped off, your vote didn't count. Nyah, nyah, nyah.

In 2004, the GOP Secretary of State in Ohio, Kenneth Blackwell, said the same, though in at least one Republican county, mentally retarded folk were hired as "chad scrapers." Law professor Bob Fitrakis of Columbus State Community College said that, because of their condition, the "scrapers" could not be asked to testify in investigations.

It's easy to see if someone voted, even if their chads are hanging out. First, look for a hole. Second, run them through the vote-counting machine. Machines kick out ballots with hung chads—but run the ballot through a couple of times and the machine shakes them off. Florida blocks the rereading of ballots.

Who cares? I mean, how many ballots are spoiled this way? Are you ready for the number? In 2000, the presidency of the United States was determined by 537 Florida votes. In all, Katherine Harris rejected 181,171 ballots.

In Ohio, Ken Blackwell used every trick in the book, from rejecting ballots of the wrong thickness to eliminating three of four voting booths in minority precincts, to bend the vote.[10] But it was the horrific ninety-four thousand spoiled votes, mostly from those chad-hangin' punch-card machines, that accounted for almost all of Bush's victory there in 2000—and history repeated itself four years later.

The US press made no mention that George Bush was elected twice by chads, not voters.

Maybe you knew about Florida and Ohio, hanging chads and all that. But what about Iowa?

In 2004, ballots not counted totaled 40,537 in Iowa—four times Bush's supposed plurality of 10,059. (Half—22,573 ballots—were spoiled; the rest were deep-sixed absentees and provisional ballots.)

Bush's plurality was also lower than the "undervote" (blank ballot) in Nevada. (The "undervote" for president is not some kind of protest vote: Nevada has a "none of the above" spot on its ballot for refuseniks.)

In 2012, the uncounted vote, not the voters, could well choose our president. Or our Congress. Or both.

And Mr. Rove knows it. And he's smiling because . . .

---

10   For a full analysis of the procedural vote-gaming in Ohio in 2004, read "Kerry Won" in *Armed Madhouse* by Greg Palast, at www.BallotBandits.org.

22.

Apple Pie Apartheid

. . . The glitches, hanging chads, "undervotes," blank ballots, and "overvotes" are not random. If every voter—white or black, Democrat or Green, 99 Percent or 1 Percenter—faced the same chance of their vote "spoiling," it wouldn't matter, it would rarely change the winner.

But, believe me, spoilage isn't random. Not even close.

The US Civil Rights Commission found, in Florida, the chance of an African American losing their vote to such "spoilage" is 900 percent higher than for a white voter. Statistician Philip Klinkner, who conducted the study, tells me that Florida is sadly typical of the nation.

I used to teach statistics myself, so I did a couple more calculations: black voters cast at least 54 percent of ballots spoiled in the USA.

The "uncount" and racial disparity is at its worst in swing states where the motive to steal is highest. In New Mexico in 2004, no fewer than 16,469 missing ballots, almost exclusively found in pueblo and Hispanic precincts, swamped Bush's "victory margin" of 5,988.

As in every state (no exceptions), the uncount in New Mexico had a dark racial hue. Just one in a hundred (1.11 percent) of Anglo presidential ballots failed to record a choice. But four times as many Hispanic ballots were blank (4.42 percent), and seven times as many Native American ballots were blank (7.05 percent). But note carefully: when paper ballots are read optically, the racial difference disappears.[11]

In all, Hispanic, Native American, or black voters cast 89 percent (nearly nine out of ten) of ballots that bit the desert dust. The breakdown: 34 percent of the lost ballots were cast by Natives, overwhelmingly Democrats, and 51 percent were cast by Mexican Americans, who vote Democratic nearly two-to-one.

A Harvard University study, "Democracy Spoiled: National, State, and County Disparities in Disenfranchisement Through Uncounted Ballots," totaled the noncount in swing states.

The authors of the study, Klinkner and Berkeley Law School Dean Christopher Edley, both told me that while their report centered on "geographical" differences, what screamed at them were the racial differences. In the

---

11   Thanks to Ellen Theisen, Stanford's Dr. David Dill, and the experts of Verified Voting for those stats.

majority, the uncounted are voters of color.

In 2004, states reported to the EAC that 133,289 ballots were rejected because of overvotes (extra marks on a ballot), with the highest percentage in "predominantly Hispanic precincts," according to the commission. Almost the entire total of overvotes came from low-income (i.e., cheap machine) precints. But only half the states and counties even bother to report the number of tossed out "overvote" ballots. And blank ballots ("undervotes")? Six times as many as overvotes, and just as biased.

And that's just the spoiled vote. Add in the felon purges, citizen purges, provisional ballots rejected, rejected registrations, and all the other voter-roll legerdemain based on racial profiling, and those biased numbers above burst through the ceiling.

Total the noncount, then crank in the racial factor, and you see that our nation's elections are spoiled rotten by the Ku Klux count.

In 2012, the color of the voter, not the choice of the voter, could for a third time in a dozen years determine control of the White House.

Forget all the baloney about democracy you heard in the sixth grade from Mrs. Gordon about the Emancipation Proclamation, the Thirteenth Amendment, and the Voting Rights Act. Ballot-box apartheid remains as American as apple pie.

No, we don't have voting booths marked *Black* or

Don't Cage Me, Bro!

In September 2007, a student at the University of Florida in Gainesville confronted Senator John Kerry with what the *Washington Post* called a "mysterious yellow book." The student, Andrew Meyer, kept demanding that Kerry explain why, given that the book proved that uncounted votes in Ohio determined the 2004 election, Kerry did not demand a full count. The kid was thrown on the ground and shocked with enough electricity to kill a weaker man, despite pleading, "Don't Tase me, bro!"

Kerry ducked and wove by saying that, yes, he'd read the strange yellow book, *Armed Madhouse* by Greg Palast.

That chapter is called "Kerry Won" and you can download it free in its entirety at www.BallotBandits.org.

Kerry never did answer the question.

White. Rather, we have voting machines for black, brown, and red precincts, along with counting and registration systems very different for light-skinned and dark-skinned Americans.

And it's not just "spoiled" votes. Of the nine ways America loses six million votes and voters, every one, *every one*, disproportionately takes away the vote of people of color.

You've got to be asking yourself, *Why have Democrats not demanded the count of the missing votes?*

Even President John Kennedy was deeply reluctant to end segregated voting. In 1963 he hesitated in the face of a personal plea in the Lincoln Room by Martin Luther King.

JFK had good (or at least, political) reasons not to act. When President Lyndon Johnson gave us the Voting Rights Act, he predicted that this would cost the Democratic Party the once-solid South. It's the sad truth that this is exactly what happened. So God bless America.

Johnson's gutsy move didn't quell Democrats' squeamishness to take on the separate-and-unequal access to the vote. Jimmy Carter relied heavily on the cracker vote and today supports that new Jim Crow tool, voter ID requirements. (Carter wears a white smile, not a white hood, so it's okay.)

There's another side to the Democrats' seemingly odd reluctance to address the apartheid voting system: Democrats are some of the worst abusers of racially loaded voting trickery.

Why? Why, when minority voters, poor voters, students, and the elderly vote strongly Democratic, would "their" party spoil, purge, block, and toss out their votes?

Because all vote theft, like all politics, is *local*. New Mexico's former Secretary of State Rebecca Vigil-Giron and former Governor Bill Richardson, each indicted in separate cases, are both Hispanic Democrats. Both did their damned best to ignore then actively deny votes to poor Hispanics and Native Americans. It goes back to state politics, where the Democratic Party's conservative and wealthy elite does whatever it takes to keep political power out of the hands of the poor.

Pecos Paul Maez and other Hispanic voters were purged by Hispanic politicians. Why? "It's on the down-low," Election Supervisor Maez told me, and wouldn't elaborate. But Hector Balderas, the state auditor, whose *mother* was purged along with *half* the voters of Mora County, almost every one Hispanic, told me they were vulnerable because Mora is dirt poor.

Voting rights attorney Santiago Juarez, now state counsel for the League of United Latin American Citizens (LULAC), who spends much of his time fighting Hispanic disenfranchisement by Hispanic politicians, explained it:

> *"You take away people's health insurance and you take their right to union pay scale, and you take away their pensions. Taking away their vote is just one more thing."*[12]

---

12   Meet Pecos Paul, Santiago Juarez, Hector Balderas, and the Acoma Pueblo leaders in the film *Billionaires & Ballot Bandits* at www.BallotBandits.org.

23.

It's Magic!

Here's an easy way to spoil a vote: digitize it . . . then lose the digits.

Prestidigitation is the French-derived term for conjury, legerdemain, sleight-of-hand, presto-change-o hand-jive, disappearing trickery . . . or, in the language of Karl Rove, "Helping America Vote."

Following what the media called the "Florida debacle," the winners of the debacle agreed to "reform" the voting system. So the Bush administration proposed and Congress passed the Help America Vote Act.

The best way to *prevent* voting reform is to pass a voting reform bill—especially if it's written by the folks that helped themselves to your vote in the first place.

The Help America Vote Act is not the most Orwellian named, satanic law ever passed by Congress, but it tries. To avoid ballots with hanging chads, the law simply does away with ballots, providing about $4 billion in subsidies for Direct Recording Equipment (DREs), better known

PRESTIDIGITIZING: The art of making votes vanish into the ether by employing paperless computer "DREs," direct recording devices, or "black boxes."

Not to be confused with votes changed via sophisticated software hacking, simple "glitches" that caused the computers to break down or simply fail to record the vote caused over half a million (546,000) votes to disappear in 2008. In 2012, expect even more to vanish.

This little-glitch-here, little-glitch-there pattern has the odd attribute that it occurs 491 percent more often in Hispanic precincts than white precincts, and in black precincts it's worse.

Presto! And it's gone!

as "computer ballots" or "black box voting."

Computer voting machines have a lot in common with slot machines in Vegas. You pull the lever and the result is, you hope, a happy one. Except that slot machines are scrupulously honest, well regulated, and operate properly and transparently.

Now, you're probably expecting me to tear off into a screed about how easy it is to fiddle with a computerized voting machine (it is), how there's rarely a "paper trail" to verify your vote (there isn't one), how the software can be hacked, cracked, hijacked, and name Donald Duck to Congress or Chuck Hagel to the US Senate. (Republican Senator Hagel, who founded the biggest voting machine company, ES&S, was elected with an astonishing number of African American votes, his skeptical Democratic opponent told me, right after his machines were installed. Obviously, a sore loser. Or sore winner. We'll never know which.)

I once suggested to President Hugo Chavez of Venezuela that if he didn't like US foreign policy, he should buy into a voting machine company. So, his buddies did just that.

But I'm *not* going to talk about the vulnerability of these "black box" machines to hacking and unknown software manipulation.

First, because there are smarter experts than me who can do a better job of explaining it. (Please read the reports of Professors David Dill of Stanford University, Steven Freeman of the University of Pennsylvania, and the stellar reportage of Brad Friedman, who have agreed to place some of their fine investigations on our site, www.BallotBandits.org.)

I've picked up from them that the good news is you may not lose your vote in the 2012 election. In fact, you may have already voted—and in November they'll tell you whom you voted for.

And that's the problem: we don't know yet how to trace the problem.

So, instead, I'm going to tell you about the *known* ways black boxes have stolen elections. And it doesn't take a Stanford math professor to figure it out.

The number one way to steal computer votes in America is to *unplug the computer.*

And dumb-ass variants thereof. The problem with computers is that *they don't work*. At least not for voters.

Example: In Sarasota in 2006, Republicans held on to the congressional seat vacated by Katherine Harris by a mere 369 votes after new computerized voting machines simply failed to record a choice in the race on eighteen thousand ballots, mostly from Democratic precincts.

The Republican county elections supervisor claimed that the eighteen thousand voters simply didn't want to make a choice. It was the top, hottest race on the ballot; eighteen thousand drove to the polls, went in, then walked out without making a choice. Oddly, this seemed to happen among voters marked *BLA* in the records, as opposed to the *WHI* voters.

There's always the innocent explanation, which is never, in fact, innocent. In some Florida precincts, the *BLA* precincts, poll workers were given the wrong passwords for the machines so no one could vote.

In a tight contest in Georgia, Diebold machines simply refused to operate and record votes in several black precincts. According to the company, the machines don't work well in very humid, hot conditions. "Well, what do you think we get in Georgia in July!" the losing candidate, Congresswoman Cynthia McKinney, told me. In the white precincts, voting was held in air-conditioned suburban school gyms.

While the software varies from maker to maker, all DRE computer voting machines have one thing in common: like the man who shot the Florida youngster

Trayvon Martin, voting machines *are really afraid of black folk*. And brown folk.

Theron Horton, a Taos-based data analyst who assists the Election Defense Alliance, has discovered that Hispanics who vote on electronic DREs are 491 percent more likely to have their vote disappear.

And Native Americans? Computers just *hate* them, just don't want them to vote. The nonvote rises by over 1,000 percent for Natives who vote on DREs versus votes spoiled on paper ballots.

How does this happen? Simple. Low-income towns get crappy schools, crappy hospitals, crappy police service, crappy everything. It would be absurd to think they'd get anything but the crappy voting machines.

When I went to the Taos Pueblo, they were voting on ancient Shouptronic machines that should have been in the Smithsonian. We don't give Natives used blankets with smallpox bugs anymore, just the used voting machines with mechanical bugs.

Even when the better machines are funded by the state, the training is lacking, the conditions of operation suck (see Georgia summer above), et cetera, et cetera.

It's that class war thing again. And in America, class is race.

Is it deliberate?

If you know it's going on and you don't change it, it's deliberate.

That's the word from the dean of county elections supervisors in Florida, Ion Sancho, the only nonpartisan election official in the state. He runs the elections in whiter-than-white Leon County, home of the state capital, Tallahassee.

He let me try out the machine he set up for Leon voters: a paper ballot that is electronically read. I voted for Ralph Nader and Pat Buchanan for president. That is, I deliberately "overvoted" (voted for two candidates for one office), spoiling it. When I stuck my ballot in the reader, it spit it back at me and told me I voted for both a consumer advocate and a pinhead bigot and had to choose one. In other words, *I couldn't spoil my ballot.* I got another ballot and made the correction.

In Sancho's last presidential election, there was *not one spoiled ballot* in his entire huge county.

Hot damn! If Florida officials knew about these machines, there would not have been 179,855 hanging chads and overvotes in 2000.

But they did know. "I invited the secretary of state to look at these machines," he said, "*before* the election." Harris could see Sancho's office from her window in the State Capitol Building. She just had to take the elevator down, or jump.

She didn't jump, nor did she take the elevator, even after Sancho told her of a deadly urgent problem. The county next door, Gadsden, the poorest and blackest in Florida, had also installed these cool miracle ballot-readers but could only afford a couple of them, which were kept in a central office. The result: the machines would reject all "spoiled" ballots—but by then the voters were far away and long gone.

Sancho realized that this would disenfranchise a massive number of poor voters in that county. It did: the blackest county in Florida had the highest spoilage rate of all.

Harris refused to fix it beforehand and refused to correct it afterward. (For example, this is where I saw ballots rejected by the machine because many voters had written-in "Al Gore." The ballot required it, but the machine couldn't read it—and Harris wouldn't count it.)

Why the heck am I reaching back to another story about Katherine Harris? Because she was the test run, the model for the rollout of the program nationwide.

That case of the eighteen thousand votes the machines didn't record in Sarasota six years later? The voters of that county voted to *ban* paperless computer voting—but the GOP county supervisor deliberately ignored the voters' will. Then he bought the paperless machines that took away their will forever.

While Florida does not permit felons to vote, robot voting machines can, and as often as they like.

With all that money to Help America Vote, you'd think the USA would be holding elections using the in-precinct, no-spoilage-possible, paper-ballot optical reader. As Sancho points outs, the fancy-pants paperless computers cost *five times as much* as the optical reader and produce *twenty times* as many spoiled ballots as Sancho's lower-tech cheapie.

So why spend *more* money to get a machine that doesn't work? Colorado's state voting task force attorney Hultin suggested one answer to me. "It's very disturbing," he said. "This law was corruptly influenced. Jack Abramoff who was a lobbyist for Diebold, the largest manufacturer of electronic vote machines. He's in prison—and [Congressman] Bob Ney who was the Chairman of the Government Operations Committee, is in prison for selling favors to Jack Abramoff in connection with [the Help America Vote] Act. So a subsidy went out: $1.5 billion to subsidize purchases of Diebold machines."

So?

"Their software loses votes." Hultin paused. "Systematically."

So?

"So," said the conservative official, "connect the dots."

Oh. Hultin said they found, and Diebold admitted, that votes are lost when the memory cards are removed from machines to gather the tally. It simply looks like "undervote," or spoilage, to the counters. Again, this is not about switching votes from one candidate to another, but the subtle, nastier method, the untraceable "glitch." But glitches that seem to occur overwhelmingly in Black, Brown, and Bluish precincts.

But the question remains: So why spend more money to get a machine that doesn't work? If you don't know the answer by now, you're not paying attention. Paperless DREs *do work perfectly . . . for those who buy the machines.*

Remember Paul Weyrich's command to the faithful: We don't want everyone to vote. Nor do we want to count their votes. And if you can get a Ku Klux robot to do the job, price is no object.

24.

The Placebo Ballot

It seems to me that someone really didn't want Hispanic votes counted, or black votes counted, and *really, really* didn't want Native votes counted.

Back at the Acoma Pueblo, the residents had a concern beyond their kids getting shot up in Iraq. (While Native Americans roundly disparage foreign wars, they are often the first to volunteer.)

South of Albuquerque, about two hundred miles from Nowhere, the pueblo lands don't look like they could support an awful lot of agriculture or ranching.

It wasn't always that way, but the runoff from the nearby uranium mines pretty much poisoned the land—and undoubtedly the Acoma people, though no one bothers to measure that.

The land is poisoned but not dead—not yet. However, there's a new worldwide uranium rush happening. So county officials, and owners of the mineral rights (not the pueblo, of course), want in on the action.

The Acoma call the resource-laced mountain above them their Mother. "She's sacred to us," Acoma elder David Ballo said. And sacred to the bottom lines of the mining companies that want to drill into her.

The big mining company out West is BP, which has gone "Beyond Petroleum"—*way* beyond petroleum. The Piute tribe is suing the company for poisoning their drinking water with uranium, and the Ute Indians are suing BP for stealing their oil à la Koch. But I digress. Surely BP would not harm Mother Mountain.

But America being a democracy, it would be put to a vote. As the tally of those who would be poisoned by the result is higher than those who would poison them, it seemed like the county board would go with leaving Mom alone.

But then the pueblo got the "Pecos Paul" treatment. You remember Pecos, the Hispanic elections supervisor who found the state purged his own registration.

The massive purge of voter rolls in Hispanic areas turned into a civil-rights massacre in the pueblos. Without notice, voters were barred for using "fake" addresses like, "near the pueblo church," which is not fake in Indian country. They needed "postal street numbers" that didn't exist.

The result: two hundred in the Acoma Pueblo showed up at the polls only to find their names purged—*poof!*

Not to worry! The voters were each given a "provisional" ballot.

A *what?*

■ ■ ■

After Katherine Harris's faux felon-purge in Florida, the Congressional Black Caucus demanded a way for wrongfully purged voters to still get their ballot.

Karl Rove agreed. *Not* a good sign.

So the Bush administration invented the "provisional" ballot. If your name doesn't appear on the voter registry, you can ask for a provisional ballot.

A better term would be "placebo" ballot. It makes you *think* you voted, but you haven't.

I spoke with John Brakey of AUDIT-AZ. The poll-watching group filed complaints in 2004 with the Arizona Secretary of State after Brakey witnessed several poll workers forcing voters to vote on provisional ballots. Mr. Brakey, these wouldn't be, uh, *Latino* voters, would they? "The poll workers were asking people their names and checking the list. One voter had the name *Juarez*. The poll workers looked it up as a *W*—and then pushed him over to a provisional."

Arizona responded by putting an end to the practice— that is, an end to the poll watching. Brakey was arrested in 2008 while monitoring a polling station.

The Congressional Black Caucus voted for HAVA. They won legal voters the right to get a provisional ballot—*but, unfortunately, not the right to have it counted.*

In Florida, I met Willie Steen—hospital orderly,

father, and felon. Well, actually, he's not a felon, but Katherine Harris listed him as one because some guy named William *O'Steen* had committed a crime. In Harris's defense, it was an easy mix-up because, despite having different names, both were listed as *BLA* in her database.[13]

Anyway, Steen took his five-year-old boy to the polling place to show him how democracy worked. The lesson was instructive. They told Steen's son that because of daddy's criminal record, he couldn't vote. Steen, who never had even a parking ticket, could now ask for a provisional ballot, and the record could be checked.

And indeed, once they check the record, they'd find he'd been wrongly listed as a felon. And so his provisional ballot *would not be counted.* There is zero provision for correcting the errors that lead to the purge in the first place.

In 2008, well over 2.1 million US citizens were given provisional ballots because they were not legal voters (felons, aliens, the insane, had fraudulent voting addresses, etc.). Given that illegal voting is a go-to-jail crime, America is apparently in the grip of a crime wave involving millions of ne'er-do-wells.

And how many arrests for the criminal attempts to vote with provisional ballots? Uh, zero. Zero out of a million

---

13   Meet Willie Steen in the BBC Television broadcasts, *Bush Family Fortunes* and *Election Files,* available for a donation to the not-for-profit Palast Investigative Fund. If you find the monkey entertaining, feed it.

supposedly illegal voters. (They are easy to find: they sign their names on the provisional ballot, a second crime.)

But maybe, just *maybe,* these are not criminals but *victims* of a crime: the crime of deliberately preventing citizens from voting.

But they *could* be criminals. We know that because most of them are *BLA* or *HISP.*

Now, let's get back to the Acoma Pueblo where the poisoned are facing off at the ballot box with the poisoners. Two hundred received provisional ballots and sent them to the county clerk, a pro-poison politician.

He rejected every single one of them.

And for good reason: *they were not sealed in official provisional ballot envelopes.*

And for good reason: *the clerk never sent the pueblo the official provisional ballot envelopes.*

Captain Iglesias didn't like the smell of that. The US attorney swooped down and brought a federal complaint against the county officials for disenfranchising the Native Americans.

The officials, by the way, were all Democrats.

But Karl Rove was, apparently, not at all pleased. Here was the proof of vote fraud and a bust of corrupt Democrats, but to Republican Party officials this was not the job Iglesias was sent to do.

The problem was that Iglesias was not supposed to bust officials defrauding voters—he was supposed to bust the *voters.*

Captain Iglesias didn't get it. So they got *him*.

Question: Pueblo Indians are Democrats through and through. Why did Democrats steal votes from Democrats? Why do so many ballots disappear in America? And, why, weirdly, so many from Indian reservations?

Follow the money. Follow the Koch Oil truck and the BP drill bits.

You can't siphon off someone's oil, nor poison their kids, nor take away their land and life and liberty unless you take away their vote.

Here is the key to understanding vote suppression:

No One Steals Votes to Win an Election.

Every crime requires two elements: motive and opportunity. Opportunity is *how* it's done. Motive is *why* it's done.

So *why* steal votes, spoil ballots, purge registrations? Don't tell me, "To steal elections." Well, *duh!* That's like saying a safe-cracker's motivation is to

TOSSING Provisional Ballots: A creature of the Help America Vote Act. When a citizen finds their name has been wrongly purged from the voter rolls, the voter may demand one of these "provisional" ballots. Like a placebo, the voter leaves the polling station happy, believes their vote has been counted. Once the voter is out of sight, most of these quasi-ballots are thrown out.

Ballot-tossing has a notable color scheme: Most tossers are white and most of the tossed are not.

get into a bank vault. No, the bank burglar's motive is not to get inside the vault but *to get the money out of it.*

This is crucial: When I went back to the Harvard study data, back to the raw EAC data, I found that *poor whites* do just as badly in the noncount as blacks and Hispanics. We see race in the stats because in America, skin color and poverty have an ugly correlation. But the noncount, county-by-county, leads to this uglier truth: *vote theft is class war by other means.*

Do the math: if the entire 99 percent voted, the 1 percent would not win an awful lot of elections. Democracy is the socialism of power.

Tom Paine said that. But then, they wouldn't let him vote either.

Indeed, as more African Americans and Latinos join the 1 percent, some are happy to yelp, "Tally-ho!" and join in the hunt of the poor voter.

Before Paine exiled himself to France (where they wouldn't let him vote either), he warned us about the disenfranchisement of the poor by the rich through the power of their purse:

> *"Personal rights, of which the right of voting for representatives is one, are a species of property of the most sacred kind: and he that would employ his pecuniary property, or presume upon the influence it gives him, to dispossess or rob another of his*

property or rights, uses that pecuniary property as he would use fire-arms."

In other words, when a rich guy uses his money to influence an election, it's no different than armed robbery.

25

Going Postal

"I didn't know I had to fill in the bubble."

That was the totally lame excuse of a voter who blew away the election of a Democrat as mayor of San Diego, California.

In 2004, the "Surfer Chick," Donna Frye, got the most votes for mayor of the city, but was refused office. Donna runs the surf shop on the beach (husband Skip Frye was the world surfing champ) and, concerned about real-estate sharks killing the beachfront and waters, decided to run for mayor as a write-in candidate.

In California, nearly a third of voters mail in their ballots. But four thousand of the folks who wrote in *Donna Frye* on those mail-in ballots *didn't fill in the bubble.*

Here's what the bubble looks like: o

On the ballot, there was a choice of candidates with a bubble next to their name and a space for *Write-in candidate.* You had to write in *Donna Frye* and fill in the bubble next to it. (Completely fill it in, but not excessively: no *X* or check—that would disqualify you too.)

Republican election officials tossed out the four thousand ballots with Frye's name but no bubble-blackening. Though Donna complained, she told me she conceded ballots marked *Surfer Chick.*

In the days when we still had a democracy, courts held that the voter's intent should determine if a ballot gets counted. But since *Bush v. Gore,* what the voter clearly wants isn't worth a bubble.

But the Rovearians insist that this is the only way to prevent wholesale fraud.

All over the nation, party hacks are playing "gotcha" with mail-in ballots. Here are some of my favorites, each one costing several thousand folks their vote:

- Wrong envelope.
- Wrong postage.
- Questionable signature.
- Stray mark (spoilage).
- Folded wrong.
- Lost by election officials.
- And an *X* instead of a dot in the bubble.

The "wrong signature" is the most suspect of all. If an election official thinks a signature has been forged, then he should *call the cops.* This is the serious crime of ballot fraud (filling out and mailing a ballot which is not yours). This is one of the only voting crimes that actually do occur, though it's incredibly rare. So if there's real evidence of a crime, the answer is not to toss out a ballot, toss out the evidence, but to jail the criminal.

So I went to visit two of the fraudsters who didn't fill in their bubbles. Maybe I'd have them busted.

"Mom! Why didn't you fill in the bubble?!"
"I'm sorry! I didn't know you had to fill in the bubble! Your sister's a lawyer and she helped us fill it out."

In the last presidential election, over twenty-seven thousand "suspicious" (i.e., forged) signatures were detected. And yet not one of these forgers was busted. Why? Maybe because they weren't forgeries but merely a slight change in signature (remember Melissa Tais?) or the pen used. Or the election official doesn't like the choices of the signatory. *Heavens! Could such a thing happen in America?*

There is a solution: if an "absentee" ballot has an error or questionable signature, the election clerks could simply call the voter and have them come in to correct it. Oregon does that. So does . . . well, actually, *no* other state does that. Because Rove and his fellow tossers want it that way.

So you lose your vote. And here's the charm: *you don't even know it! Ha ha ha!*

Does it matter?

It has more than once changed "Hail to the Chief" to "Hail to the Thief."

In 2012, it is expected that about 26 million votes will be mailed in. And, in the name of preventing voter fraud, about ONE IN FOURTEEN WILL BE TOSSED OUT. That's nearly *two* million votes tossed in the *gotcha!* dumpster.

But don't both parties do it, play "gotcha" with the ballots? Yes, they do. So then it all evens out, right? *Wrong!*

If you've been paying attention,

REJECTING Absentee or Mail-in Ballots:

About 26 million absentee ballots will be mailed in to partisan election supervisors in November 2012. Records indicate about one in fourteen, or nearly two million, will be thrown out for wrong postage, wrong envelope, wrong signature (middle initial added or missing), being folded wrong, or a bubble marked with an *X* instead of a dot.

you've already guessed that the probability that a mail-in ballot will get the heave-ho is based on the color of the person whose name is on the ballot and his or her income bracket.

And just to make certain the class-biased count would pick one of their candidates, the Kochs spent at least a million on absentee ballot handling in the June 2012 Wisconsin gubernatorial recall race. Using their new monster database, Republicans received a preprinted ballot and envelope with all the personal data properly filled-in to make it reject-proof. Just sign and drop in a mailbox.

It's legal and brilliant. What's brilliant and possibly not so legal is that in November, the same database could be "inverted" to target the Blue-ballot absentee voters and do the same match for the purpose of pumping up rejections and challenges. They won't? During the recall, a group called United Sportsmen of Wisconsin sent Democrats absentee ballot request forms with the wrong address and deadline. USW, which existed only during the Wisconsin recall, was created by John W. Conners—until recently, Director of the Kochs' Americans for Prosperity. That's sportsmanship a la Koch.

26.

Block the Vote

It's lookin' bad for the old white guys. Besides the 16 million ex-cons who can vote but don't know it, there's about *eleven million* Hispanic citizens unregistered, Americans all, and fifteen million kids between the ages of eighteen and twenty-four who can't be pried away from Facebook long enough to register—at least so the tally of vote registries say. These unvoters, if they suddenly registered, could rock the planet.

You think the Old World Order hasn't thought of that?

So, then, how do they stop Americans from taking over America? Easy: *first, make registering voters a crime.*

In a swing state like Florida with its huge new Hispanic population (no, not Cubans, Puerto Ricans), you make it *illegal* to register citizens at welfare offices, churches, or voter-registration drive meetings. (Suggestion: sneak voter registration forms into handgun barrels. Guns are allowed at all these locations.)

Second, make registering voters as risky as a derivative from JPMorgan. In Florida (I love using Florida for vote-suppression examples, don't you?), Governor Jeb Bush made it a crime, with vicious fines, to turn in voter forms more than forty-eight hours after they were gathered, or with itty-bitty errors in them. He successfully put the League of Women Voters out of the registration business until June 2012 when a judge enjoined Florida from sentencing registrars to hard time. But with ACORN's corpse still fresh, the League and others remain fearful of going into the streets of Miami with clipboards.

Still, why is the Hispanic registration rate so absolutely dismal?

According to the *New York Times,* it's first and foremost the Latinos' "entrenched pattern of nonparticipation." In other words, they're just lazy, don't give a taco, and treasure their siesta more than their vote. Nowhere in the long, front-page article does the *Times* writer veer from the racial profile of Chicanos as unengaged if not hostile to registering to vote.

If the *Times* checked the stats instead of relying on stereotypes from an old Cantinflas movie, it could have found from the detailed survey by the US Census Bureau that *white* voters are one-third more likely than Hispanic voters to say they don't register because of disinterest.[14]

---

14   Indeed, the statistical survey shows Hispanics the most committed of any ethnic group to *attempting* to register. While the *Times* article tediously quotes those Hispanics who say their vote won't make a difference, the Census shows that *whites* express that view twice as frequently as Hispanics (http://www.census.gov/prod/2010pubs/p20-562.pdf).

The biggest problem identified by Hispanic citizens them-selves in registering is "difficulty in English." D'oh! The *Times no piense de eso, los chingates.*

But there's another explanation for the *drop* in Hispanic registration: Hispanics *do* register, by the millions—only to have their registration forms rejected, or, if they sneak onto the rolls, have their names purged. Nothing about the Purge'n General Donetta Davidson removing one in five Colorado voters from the registry made it to the attention of the *Times*.

The *Times*, if their reporters weren't too lazy to check the facts, would find out that *the majority of registration forms submitted by legal voters of color in California had been rejected.*

For several years, Hispanics have filled out the forms and the state has thrown them out.

It was the Republican Secretary of State Bruce McPherson who rejected nearly half (42 percent) of new registrations out of hand in California, over fourteen thousand voters in LA County alone. (He didn't, by the way, bother to tell the voters. He wanted to make it a sur-prise on Election Day.)

Only the County of Los Angeles questioned this alleged avalanche of phony voters. The county called each rejected voter and every one reached was in fact legit, but their names were input wrong by the state clerks or simply rejected as "suspicious" to the GOP official. (NB: Asians

vote Democratic, and their registration rates are worse than for Hispanics.)

And that's yet another way to kill your registration: about 2.2 million names have been misspelled or contain other errors *made by government clerks*. McPherson's replacement Bowen told me that they couldn't handle the hyphenated and unfamiliar spellings of new voters; but the GOP officials tagged clerical errors of the state as "fraud" by voters.

When the voters arrive, in most cases they'll be told, "Tough luck, Chuck!" or handed a provisional placebo ballot.

And as California goes, so goes the nation. Several states now require that proof of citizenship be *mailed in* with the form. Dear reader, do you have proof of citizenship that matches your registration name, signature, and address?

It's crazy, but only two states, Maine and Michigan, have more than 50 percent of eligible Hispanic citizens registered. Michigan's former Governor Jennifer Granholm told me that was only possible because she teamed with the NAACP to fight the Republicans' creepy purge campaign. (See Chapter 31, "Wiped Away in 8 Mile.")

Yes, there are fewer Hispanics and African Americans on voter rolls than in 2008, but it's not for lack of trying. With 20 million registrations purged *each year* under the Help America Vote Act, plus the massive rejections, plus the state errors, it's surprising that there are any voters of color left at all.

Those who attempt to register get defeated in an impossible game of chutes-and-ladders, a maze with trap doors and lions and tigers and bears. In the swing state of Indiana (we'll get there), new ID laws have kept three out of four Hispanic citizens from registering.

And despite the federal law requiring states to make voter registration forms available at government offices, in some states like Florida, the papers have been yanked from welfare offices and *outlawed* in high schools.

It's worked damn well too. The number of voting citizens with incomes less than $15,000 has actually declined. Mission Accomplished! In Florida, registration is down by eighty-one thousand in May 2011 compared to May 2008.

So get ready for the bottom line: the number of black and Hispanic registered voters in the USA has fallen radically since 2008, by two million in these four years.

The Obama campaign, squeamish about making race an issue, is literally in denial—casting doubt on the US Census registry figures—rather than confronting the cybernetic resurrection of Jim (and José) Crow.

And that's why, by the way, I'm telling you to *steal back your vote* yourself. Relying on political parties didn't work for Martin Luther King, and he won a Nobel Prize. You have to defend yourself, not wait for a politician to protect you. (Self-defense weaponry listed at the back of this book: *7 Ways to Beat the Ballot Bandits* and resource groups.)

But let's consider the strange notion that Hispanic registration is falling because *the illegal aliens on the voter rolls are running back over the border, back to Mexico.*

In the swing state of Arizona, that is the official line. (Warning: while other states have official flowers, Arizona has official delusions. It's the heat.) Anyway, about a hundred thousand Hispanics have had their names removed from the voter rolls in Arizona, and *Rolling Stone* thought I should go catch a couple of these aliens in the act of voting.

27

Aliens Attack!

"There is a massive effort underway to register illegal aliens in this country!"
—State Senator Russell Pearce

Arizona State Senator Russell Pearce sponsored one of the nation's nastiest ID laws, Prop 200. It requires all new registrants to prove they are US citizens.

When I heard about all these illegal aliens wading the Rio Grande, I had to call Senator Pearce's office.

"How many illegal aliens have actually been registered?" I asked.

Pearce's PR flak told me, *five million.* All Democrats too.

FIVE MILLION? *WOW!!* Our investigations team flew to Arizona to look for these hordes of voters swimming the Rio Grande—just so they could vote for Obama.

We wanted Pearce to give us their names and addresses so we could bust a bunch and get a Pulitzer Prize. It should be easy: their names and addresses are on their felonious registration forms. I'd happily make a citizen's arrest of each one, on camera. But Pearce ducked us, literally hiding from our cameras. Turns out, he didn't have five million names. He didn't have *five*. He didn't have *one*.

His five million alien voters came from a Republican website that extrapolated from the number of Mexicans in a border town who refused jury service because they were not citizens. Not one, in fact, had registered to vote: they had registered to *drive*. They had obtained licenses as required by the law.

The illegal voters, "wetback" welfare moms, and alien job-thieves are just GOP website wet-dreams, but their mythic

PR power helps the party's electoral hacks chop away at voter rolls and civil rights with little more than a whimper from the Democrats.

There are only four proofs of citizenship in the USA:

1. If you have your original birth certificate. Good luck with that, especially among the Hispanic poor who had home births and little access to such records.

2. A US passport. (Not many of the clerks working at Wal-Mart look like they'd just come back from their ski vacation in the Alps.)

3. Naturalization papers. If you become a citizen, you have documents that say so. The problem is that most Hispanic families in Arizona were citizens of the USA before there was a USA. They are natural, not naturalized, citizens, and so don't have the papers.

4. White skin. In Arizona, according to the US Justice Department, the cops accept that white skin is a proof of citizenship. Maricopa County (Phoenix) Sheriff Joe Arpaio is on trial for having his cops stop citizens of brownish hue, demanding their citizenship papers and tossing them in the hooskow when they don't.

I tested the white-skin-is-citizenship rule myself. I went to visit Arpaio's famous (infamous?) open-air prison in the desert. You can see the sign, ILLEGAL ALIENS ARE PROHIBITED FROM VISITING ANYONE IN THIS JAIL—SHERIFF JOE ARPAIO. What if he found out that Grandma Palast snuck in from Windsor, Canada!

Not to worry: the sheriff's crew was happy to escort me and my investigations chief around Tent City, and the deportee-sniffing professionals never asked for her citizenship papers. She doesn't have them because she's not a citizen. But she did remember to bring her white skin.

But hunting for illegal aliens isn't the point. Arizona Hispanics vote two-to-one Democratic and if they were all allowed to register, the Republican sheriff and the state GOP would be toast. Or, I should say, tortillas.

And it's darn effective. So far, not one illegal alien has been caught voting—but *one in three* registrations in Phoenix have been rejected.

Olé, Señor Rove!

28

I'm De-Pressed

I hope you're asking, *Why haven't America's own daily papers and news networks led these investigations?*

I suspect it's partly the magic-show thing. No one inside the Great American Circus Tent likes to believe they're being fooled. America likes to think of itself as a democracy. No one really wants to know their ballot has gotten hijacked, boosted, deep-sixed, caged, purged, stuck inside a robot's pocket, fiddled, filched, flimmed, or flammed.

When Katherine Harris purged tens of thousands of innocent black voters as felons in 2000, BBC put it right at the top of the prime-time news, and the *Guardian* newspaper on its front page. All over the world, headlines screamed about the Fix in Florida—except in the US, where the story was on page *nothing*.

I have to admit that the *New York Times* did editorialize against "Florida manipulating voter rolls to purge felons . . . removing black voters who were not felons." But the *Times* published that comment about the 2000 election *in 2012*. A decade earlier, the Paper of Record flat-out refused the story from the *Guardian*. CBS News also declined to run the BBC story because, Dan Rather's producer told me, the story "didn't stand up." CBS's investigation consisted of: *"We called Jeb Bush's office."* Bush's PR flunky told CBS that our BBC story was wrong. And for CBS News, that was good enough.

You can't make this up.

I have neither sufficient time, space, nor alcohol to enumerate the failings of what is laughably called "news reporting" in the USA. But I have to mention at least four *-isms* that scare away America's press from covering the finagling of the vote:

1. Lazy-ass-ism.
2. Phony "balance"-ism.
3. Fear of journalism.
4. Racism.

Let me illustrate from the *best* in American reporting:

In May 2012, National Public Radio announced that Governor Rick Scott had ordered a purge of 182,000 "noncitizens" from Florida voter rolls. In one of those deep and self-serious voices used by NPR reporters, we were told:

> *"Republican leaders say the new voting rules are needed to combat fraud. Recently, state elections*

*officials began an investigation that appears to give
that argument some credence. They announced
they're examining registrations of thousands of
Florida voters who may not be US citizens. The
chairman of Florida's Republican Party, Lenny
Curry, says the investigation shows why tighter
voting rules are necessary."*

Okay, class: What is the credible evidence, the facts
reviewed by NPR, that give "some credence" to the accu-
sation that over a hundred thousand aliens are registered?

One would think that "credence" would mean finding
illegal voters. No one has yet found a single one as of this
writing. Certainly not NPR, which blessed the Republican
voter-roll purge list—*without obtaining a copy of the list.*

NPR was quick to balance its conclusion that the list
was, in part, credible, with a statement that "voting
rights activists say the investigation is an attempt by a
Republican administration to bolster the legal case for the
restrictions."

Well, is it or isn't it? Are there illegal alien voters or not?
If you are an NPR listener all you got was a load of he-said,
she-said, and a pitch for a coffee mug.

*Wow! Illegal aliens! From Mexico? From Mars? From
Andromeda?*

NPR won't say because NPR's ace reporter didn't, uh,
look at the list.

The Paper of Record, the *New York Times,* delved deeper:

> *"Some of the people on an initial list of 2,700 possible noncitizens sent to county election supervisors were either naturalized citizens or were born in the United States."*

Some people? Did the *Times* go through the list? *Nyet.*

By saying "some," the *Times* implicitly endorses the idea that the purge list is mostly accurate. Indeed, the headline, "Florida Steps Up Effort Against Illegal Voters," gives the conclusion that there *are* illegal voters, and even, in liberal high dudgeon, when the paper questions the purge, it states the purge list "may well include legitimate voters."

"May?" MAY???

There ain't no "may" about it. Aliens registering or voting have committed a felony crime punishable by imprisonment *and* deportation. The attorney general of Florida says he'll arrest every one—if, in fact, they are lawbreakers. Out of the 182,000 illegal alien voters in the "crime wave," Florida has scooped up exactly *none.*

I've made this public promise: if 182 criminal voters are found, *just one in a thousand*, I will chew Governor Scott's shorts in the Capitol rotunda. So far, I have not been invited to dine.

US Attorney Iglesias said of the similar alien witch-hunt ordered by Karl Rove in New Mexico that he ran all over the mesas and couldn't find one. Not one.

So who is on the Florida list? Like the ones in several other states, it is a brilliant manipulation of data-matching algorithms. Playing on the flaws in data sets, GOP officials are able to gin up "suspects" for a crime not committed. It's brilliant because in a state where whites make up 74 percent of the voter rolls, the purge list is 74 percent black and Hispanic. Hmmm.

So the game is played skillfully by the vote snatcher: the US media accepts on its face that there are millions of illegal voters nationwide; aliens so wily and devious and talented that even though they present themselves in person, and list their addresses, they are never caught.

For the media, the only issue is whether the *method* used to hunt down these phantoms is fair or not. So, the *Times* concludes:

> *"No process is perfect," said Lenny Curry, the chairman of the Republican Party in Florida. "That doesn't mean there shouldn't be a process and you shouldn't try to protect the system."*

Why don't we get the full story? That the lists are nearly 100 percent bullshit and crafted as such deliberately?

Let's go back to the four *-isms*. First, the US media *hates hates hates* to take the time, energy, and expense to actually hunt down the evidence and review it. "Lazy-ass-ism" is not necessarily the choice of reporters but a limit imposed by greedy-ass networks and producers afraid of taking a position on the facts.

A production team from *60 Minutes* visited our office during our 2004 BBC investigation of vote suppression, asking to join with us. When we produced the actual purge lists, the CBS producer exclaimed, *"Why, you'd have to spend a hundred hours going through that list!"*

Well, no shit, Sherlock.

It's much cheaper and easier to just report competing accusations, *he-said, she-said.* In place of news, we get, "Karl Rove says that the moon is made of cheese and stolen ballots and the ACLU says that's not totally accurate."

That's called a "balanced" report.

It would not be "balanced," however, to say the lists are *deliberately* created to have a Jim Crow profile. BBC gave me *months* to hunt the evidence. And when I found the smoking guns showing that the racial attack on innocents was deliberate, budgeted with millions of tax dollars, BBC required me to confront the Florida secretary of state's purge director, Clayton Roberts, with the evidence. When I did, he ripped off his microphone, ran into his office (with me running behind), locked the door, and called in the state troopers to have me and my camera crews frog-marched out of the capitol.

You can't show that on US television. It's considered

"advocacy" reporting. Or worse, "muckraking." Not "balanced." In the rest of the world, it's called *journalism*. Not that I'm complaining.

The *Times* and NPR are the *good* journalists. But then there's fiction, falsehood, factual flatulence, and Fox, the network that features the hysterical vote-fraud fantasies of fakers like John Fund. I don't have time to show you all the nuts in that fruitcake, but let me give you one doozy from Fund, who claims that there wasn't a single case of wrongful disenfranchisement of African American voters.

Mr. Fund, meet Mr. Steen. Gulf War veteran. Dad. Never had a parking ticket. *BLA*—and purged. Twice.

29

So These Ten Nuns Walk Into a . . .

Stop me if you heard this one. See, these ten nuns walk into a polling station in Indiana and the guy in charge says, *"Whoa, Sisters! What do think you're doing?"*

"Voting," says Sister Mary.

"Well, not here, ladies; not without your *ID!*" He demanded their driver's licenses, but the ten quite elderly Sisters of the Holy Cross, including a ninety-eight-year-old, had long ago given up cruising.

"Scram, Sis!" said the man, and kicked their habits right out of the polling station.

I may not have gotten the dialogue exactly right, but I got the gist of it and the facts: the ten nuns who'd been voting at that station for decades were booted out in 2008, just after the state of Indiana's Republican legislature imposed new voter ID laws.

The reason for nixing the nuns? To stop voter identity theft.

There wasn't exactly a voter identity crime wave. In fact, despite no photo ID requirement, *there wasn't a single known case of false identity voting in the state in over one hundred years.*

About four hundred thousand voters (9 percent of Indiana's electorate) are African American. Nearly one in five (18.1 percent) lack the ID needed to vote, according to Matt Barreto of the University of Washington. That's twice the number of whites lacking ID.

Therefore, as many as seventy-two thousand black voters will get the boot when they show up to vote this November. Coincidentally, that's three times Barack Obama's victory margin in that state in 2008. Coincidentally.

And who are the *white* folk lacking ID? The elderly, like the sisters, and students like Angela Hiss and Allyson Miller, whose official state IDs don't list their dorm room addresses and so can't be used to vote.

Black folk, the elderly, students, poor whites blocked

EJECTING: There are several ways to throw nuns, or others with a Black habit, out of a voting station. The best: require a government-approved photo ID, though school and food-stamp photo IDs are usually barred (though gun licenses will do). This is to prevent the crime of someone stealing someone else's identity to vote—a crime that in states with harsh ID laws has never happened. But it does prevent another crime: VWB—Voting While Black.

from registering and voting—a federal judge didn't think it was all that coincidental. Justice Terence Evans could see a pattern: "The Indiana voter photo ID law is a not-too-thinly veiled attempt to discourage election-day turnout by certain folks believed to skew Democratic."

But Supreme Court Justice is blind. The Indiana law does provide a voter the chance to obtain an ID from government offices. The average voter's distance to the office is seventeen miles. By definition, the folks that need the ID don't drive. And the ninety-eight-year-old is pretty darn slow in her walker.

A lawyer for Indiana voters told me that the average bus trip back and forth, requiring two changes, takes an entire work day. They tested it. But Supreme Court Justice Antonin Scalia ruled that the law was fair and provided "equal protection" to all voters because "seventeen miles is seventeen miles for the rich and the poor."

Our investigative team decided to check that assumption. Justice Scalia drives a black BMW. No kidding. What he meant to say is that whether a poor person or a rich person is driving a BMW, it takes the same time. And whether the BMW is black or white doesn't matter either.

With Supreme Court blessings, voter ID laws are taking the nation by storm, or storm troops.

Apparently, the idea came to Karl Rove while buying

his pampers. He told the Republican National Lawyers Association, "I go the grocery store and I want to cash a check to pay for my groceries, I have to show a little bit of ID. [So, why not when] it comes to the most sacred thing in our democracy?"

(Actually, Karl, you *don't* have to show ID to swallow the Eucharist or matzo. But if by "most sacred thing" in our democracy you mean making donations to American Crossroads, you don't need ID for that anymore either. If you mean *voting* is sacred, then it shouldn't be dependent on taking a driving test, should it?

Anyway, I'd love to see Rove actually cashing a check at a grocery store, especially one written by the Ice Man. But I digress.)

Santiago Juarez sees some truth in Rove's remarks. I met with Santiago in Espanola, New Mexico, where he was running a registration drive among low-riders, the young Mexican Americans who cruise the street in hopping, bopping, neon-lit Chevys. He says, "And who's going to give these kids a credit card?" Of course, you can always get ID from a state office . . . if you already have ID.

Voting-rights lawyer John Boyd, who works for both parties, is alarmed by the "thousands and thousands" of poor people in each state that will lose their vote because of new ID laws.

"I don't have any doubt this could decide the election," he told me. "People don't understand the enormity of this."

People don't. But Karl does.

And so does the Brennan Center. The Brennan Center for Justice at New York University Law School brings together America's most prestigious scholars in the field of voting rights who are widely ignored because of their unquestioned expertise. The Brennan Center reports that the ID laws are racist, ageist, classist, and the stupidest way to stop "fraud."

Here's the Brennan Center breakdown of those without government photo ID:

- 6.0 million seniors;
- 5.5 million African Americans;
- 8.1 million Hispanics;
- 4.5 million eighteen- to twenty-four-year olds; and
- 15 percent voters with household income under $35,000 a year.

Now, don't add them up because there's a lot of double-counting here. "Poor," "black," and "young" go together like "stop" and "frisk."

But let's cut to the chase: the draconian ID law and other voting and registration restrictions passed in just the year before the 2012 election, according to the Brennan

Center, are going to cause *five million voters* to lose their civil rights.

Overwhelmingly, the changes were made in twelve "battleground" states, with the most radical exclusion laws adopted in Florida and Wisconsin. The cheese-chewer state will require government-issued IDs to vote. But the IDs issued by the state itself to University of Wisconsin students won't be accepted. That's okay because, as a New Hampshire legislator, hoping to emulate Wisconsin, points out, "Kids, you know, just vote liberal."

Using a formula provided by the Brennan Center, we can calculate that 97,850 student voters were barred, turned away, blocked, challenged, or given provisional ballots (left uncounted) on recall Election Day in June. No US paper listed Wisconsin as a "swing" state that month. Well, it swung.

Altogether, the 2012 changes in Wisconsin law were sufficient alone to account for the victory of Republican Governor Scott Walker in staving off that recall vote in June 2012. Walker did have the popular support of $31 million (versus $4 million raised by his Democratic opponent).

30

Stuffed

Besides all these sophisticated new disenfranchisement devices, there remains good old-fashioned ballot-box stuffing.[15]

The good old system of filling out a bunch of blank ballots and sticking them in the box has a modern electronic twist: the proliferation of notoriously hackable electronic voting and tabulation machines can make recounts impossible. Compounding that threat to democracy is a raft of new state statutes that make it difficult to obtain hand recounts.

During the 2004 presidential contest, rural Warren County was among the last of Ohio's jurisdictions to report its vote count. Immediately after polls closed, Warren County's GOP election officials declared a terrorist alert, locked down the polling station, evicted all media observers, and trucked the ballots to a secluded

---

15   This chapter is written by Professor Kennedy.

warehouse controlled by a Republican Party official where they tallied and then retallied until they produced for Bush a suspicious fourteen thousand more votes than he had earned in 2000. The FBI subsequently acknowledged that the terrorist alert was a Republican contrivance. A *Cincinnati Enquirer* investigation proved that Republicans had planned the fabricated emergency nine days before the election.

In Baldwin County, Alabama, GOP activists used similar tactics to overturn the 2002 reelection of Governor Don Siegelman. Siegelman is best known nationally for his conviction and imprisonment under laughable charges of bribery ginned-up by a cast of crooked GOP attorneys, political operatives, and judges acting in concert with Karl Rove. (A federal judge who initially reviewed and dismissed the case urged that the Justice Department should be investigated for false prosecution; the Supreme Court overturned the dismissal.) Congressional hearings on Siegelman's case stalled over Karl Rove's refusal to testify, and the Bush White House claimed to have lost key documents. The faux bribery charge received national attention, but not this story of the theft of Siegelman's 2002 election:

STUFFING: Election officials stuff ballot boxes with ballots they've filled out.

Heavily Republican Baldwin County on the "Redneck Riviera" was one of the last Alabama counties to report results during Siegelman's hotly contested race against GOP challenger Bob Riley. At 11:00 that evening, local Republican officials huddled in the basement of the Bay Minette Courthouse, struggling with an electronic tabulator that they claimed had malfunctioned. The tabulator was supposed to count votes that had been collected from voting machines across the county. The GOP officials told Democrats and members of the press gathered outside the tabulator room that there was a "glitch," but they refused to give details. After virtually all the other counties had reported, Republican officials distributed a printout summarizing Baldwin County's election results to officials from both parties, and to Associated Press and local media reporters. The official tally had Siegelman with 19,070 votes to Riley's 31,052. The results—consistent with predictions for this Republican-dominated Gulf Coast county—meant that Siegelman had won the statewide race and would retain the governor's seat.

Republican officials then locked the courthouse for the night and sent poll watchers, the Democratic Party chairman, and the media home. Governor Siegelman gave a victory press conference and called upon Riley to concede.

Later that night, however, Republican officials posted another report on the county probate court's website reducing Siegelman's count to 12,736, a deduction of 6,334 votes. The revised tally gave Riley a margin of 3,120 votes out of 1.3 million cast, or a razor-thin victory by 0.23 of a percentage point. Tellingly, neither the lieutenant governor's race, nor any of the down-ballot contests, changed in the new tally by even a single vote.

Siegelman next plowed into the same brick wall Al Gore had encountered two years before: a system rigged by Republicans to prevent hand recounts. At eight the next morning, Wednesday, Siegelman and his supporters, attorneys, and a contingent of reporters assembled at the probate court building seeking an explanation for the sudden change in Siegelman's results. But the canvassing board—the body charged with safeguarding the election— had barred the courthouse doors from inside and refused Siegelman's team entry. The board included the probate judge, a representative from the sheriff's department, and the clerk of court—all Republicans. Finally, around 10:15 a.m., the board emerged and announced its intention to certify the election results immediately. Under the statute, the canvassing board should not have certified the result until noon Friday. Siegelman and his team pleaded with them to wait. But the canvassing board insisted that the results were correct and illegally certified the altered election results at 10:30 a.m. A half hour later, Riley delivered his victory speech in Montgomery.

In response, the Democratic Party filed recount petitions in all of Alabama's sixty-seven counties. One petition demanded a manual recount of all of Baldwin County's paper ballots.

Section 307-X-1.21 of Alabama's administrative code requires that, in the face of such requests, "the box or envelope holding the ballots shall be delivered unopened to the supervising official in charge of the re-count," and that a "recount must be conducted under the supervision of a trained and certified poll official and/or Probate Judge of the County." Faced with this unambiguous language, local Republican officials, including the sheriff and the circuit court and probate judges, all agreed to let Siegelman have a hand count of one of the precincts where large numbers of votes had been switched. That's when Republican Attorney General Bill Pryor stepped in.

Pryor threatened to jail anyone who attempted to count the ballots, citing an obscure Alabama constitution provision prohibiting the breach of a sealed ballot box in the absence of a court order. Siegelman filed the lawsuit asking the court to unseal the ballot boxes, but he already knew it was a lost cause.

It was a Karl Rove courthouse. The Business Council of Alabama had imported Rove from Texas in 1994 to mastermind a GOP takeover of the state's electoral offices, particularly its judiciary, which was perceived as unreliable by the state's corporate interests. Rove brought his rough brand of politics to the races for Alabama's appellate courts, one that soon had judicial candidates accusing each other of bribery, favoritism, and moral turpitude. It worked. The state high court went from solid Democratic to all Republican, except for one lone Democrat.

"So we were then left with filing a state lawsuit," Siegelman told us, "knowing that by that time, Karl Rove had already changed eight of the nine members of the Alabama Supreme Court, so we were facing an eight-to-one Republican majority on the State Supreme Court. Knowing what Al Gore went through, I just felt like the elections contest wasn't going to go anywhere, we were never going to get the recount that we needed, so I announced that we were going to just live to fight another day and we walked away from the contest." Siegelman threw in the towel on November 18, and Riley was sworn in as governor on January 21, 2003, at the state capitol in Montgomery. (President Bush rewarded Pryor for his accomplishments with appointment to a federal judgeship.)

"Karl Rove's fingerprints were all over this," Siegelman told us. The Alabama Republican Party, apparently proud of its acumen rather than shamed by the corruption, gave its consultant Kitty McCullough (a.k.a. Kelly Kimbrough) credit for the electronic vote switch, applauding her "for finding the votes that delivered the election to Riley." McCullough was Rove's business partner at his political consulting and direct-mail firm K. Rove & Company.

McCullough shared the credit with another of Rove's key Alabama operatives, Dan Gans. Gans, a self-described "electronic ballot security expert," had served as Riley's chief of staff during Riley's term as a US Representative for Alabama's 3rd District, before going to work on Riley's gubernatorial campaign. Not long after the election, he went to work for the Alexander Strategy Group (ASG), the Washington lobbying and consulting firm run by Rove's friend Jack Abramoff. ASG disbanded in 2006 when it was implicated in the scandal that resulted in Abramoff's imprisonment. Gans would brag on his ASG Internet bio that he "implemented a state-of-the-art ballot security program that was critical to securing governor-elect Riley's narrow margin of victory (3,120 votes)."

31.

Wiped Away in 8 Mile

In 2008, at BBC, I got a call from Detroit, which surprised me because I thought Detroit had died years ago.

I was told that banks were foreclosing on tens of thousands of homes; families were being forced from their houses in herds. And as the judge's gavel came down, sealing the foreclosures, something most interesting happened: the foreclosed residents had their names struck from the voter rolls.

It seems the Republican Party had challenged the rights of voters to cast ballots because their addresses were no longer valid, having lost their right to live where they lived. Lose your home, lose your vote. Even if they still lived in the state, or even if they had remained in the house.

What intrigued me was how the GOP got ahold of the names of those facing foreclosure. It was the summer of 2008, the world economy and General Motors had driven off a cliff, and foreclosed voters, even those who had moved away within the state, would have no time to challenge the challenge to their vote—nor even, if they mailed in their ballot, would they know their names had been removed.

BBC told me to get there and find some families facing foreclosure (an all too easy task).

I started out in the "8 Mile" neighborhood of Detroit. In the film *8 Mile*, Eminem had portrayed the place as a lower-working-class dead end, the decayed monument to America's new era of downward mobility.

But now, it is much worse. When I found the home of Robert Pratt, the street had already been bank-bombed. Four or five houses had already been foreclosed and emptied, their windows smashed out, weeds belly high, doors hanging from one hinge, leaving the street like it had been busted in the face, with half its teeth missing.

That meant that the rest of the houses would go too. They were now, in this economic death zone, nearly worthless. Pratt's home, he told me, could maybe sell for $30,000. Maybe. He owed the bank $110,000 on it.

It was a nice home, actually, a small, neat bungalow where his surviving four kids played, though not outside. (Pratt's twelve-year-old had died of a stray bullet while playing in their backyard.)

Pratt, a member of the United Auto Workers, worked seven days a week, but his pay sank and his wife lost her job with the city as Detroit's government rushed toward bankruptcy.

In the meantime, his monthly payments on the home

doubled under some truly usurious interest formula used by Bank of America's Countrywide subprime mortgage unit. With two union jobs in the family when they applied, the Pratts should not have been given the brutally costly subprime rate, but the bank, according to the records, steered nearly every black family into subprime. And now they couldn't pay the rising interest, doubling their monthly bill. So the bank's law firm, Trott & Trott, told them they had to get out of the house.

As the house was effectively worthless and no one would buy it even if the Pratts left to sleep in their car, what was the point of throwing the family out? The point was that Trott & Trott, a "mortgage mill," made a fee on each foreclosure and eviction. They did hundreds at a time.

I thought I'd check out the firm and headed off to their huge headquarters on the other side of town. It was slick, new, and several stories: business was booming. With my cameraman Rick Rowley, I was trying to figure how I could jump one of the Trotts themselves to find out about the foreclosures—and the voter-roll purges.

We pretended to film some executives, following them through the security doors, into the main lobby, and up to Mr. Trott's office. Did the Trott Brothers give their lists of properties they slated for foreclosure to the GOP?

Their answer was to call security. On the ground floor, as we stalled while getting hustled out, we saw to our left what looked like just another division of the Trott & Trott foreclosure factory. Except for a small sign that said, *John McCain for President, Michigan State Headquarters.*

Mystery solved. That was a quick investigation. Still, we slipped back in to ask if the Republican campaign was using Trott & Trott foreclosure lists to eliminate citizens' voting rights.

Their answer was expected. "You wouldn't want illegal voters to cast ballots, would you?" said a functionary. No, I wouldn't. I guess that poverty had become a crime in Michigan.

Today, Trott & Trott is legal counsel to the Mitt Romney for President campaign. The firm has tossed $100,000 into the Restore Our Future kitty for Mitty. And, so as not to create PR problems for the campaign, Trott & Trott won't foreclose on more than one thousand houses in Romney's hometown. (I made that up: foreclosures continue.)

I think of Romney's line, that "we Republicans are a party that celebrates success." When T&T boot a family of voters from a home, is the celebration of their success held upstairs in the partners' offices or on the ground floor at GOP headquarters?

All over America, foreclosure and vote loss go hand in hand, fist in claw. Take a look at this comparison of precincts of high vote loss due to "spoilage" compared to high incidence of foreclosures in Cleveland, Ohio. It's not just a matter of "lose your home, then lose your votes." These neighborhoods are weakened financially and politically. It goes together.

And it matters. You are looking at a scattergram of the

ballots spoiled and rejected that reelected George Bush in 2004. Compare it to the foreclosure diagram. God Bless America.

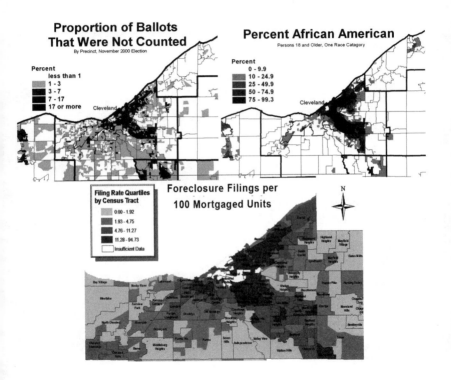

32.

Restoring the Billionaires' Future

I ran the Pratt family's story and the evidence of the purge of the impoverished on European television. But I wasn't done with the story in Detroit, of homes and votes lost. Something bothered me. So many houses empty with that *whoosh* of running water—pipes stripped out before the city can turn the water off. Why so many?

The Republican windfall, "foreclosing" on voter registrations, that's just the endgame to make sure the victims of the con don't have the political power to seek revenge.

But revenge for what?

The working class of Detroit was losing billions of dollars in wages and pensions. And one thing I know about a billion dollars—if someone loses it, someone else has found it.

And all I could think of was this: *someone wants these houses to die.* Someone wants Detroit to fall to its knees, wants Robert Pratt to stay awake at night hoping against hope to keep his bungalow in the warzone of 8 Mile.

Who would be so sick, so devious and cruel and brilliant, as to want the housing market in Michigan to die—the entire US market to?

Here's who:

In August 2007, one year before I walked into Robert Pratt's home, John Paulson walked into Goldman Sachs, the investment bank, with a billion-dollar idea. Paulson's brainstorm had all the elements that Goldman found enchanting: a bit of fraud, a bit of flimflam, and lots and lots of the ultimate drug: *OPM*—Other Peoples' Money.

Paulson's scheme was simple. Paulson, a much followed hotshot hedge-fund manager, would announce that he was betting big on the recovery of the US housing market. He was willing to personally insure that billions of shaky subprime mortgages, like the one dumped on the Pratts, would never go into default.

Now, all Goldman had to do was line up some suckers with more money than sense, some big European banks that handled public pension funds, and get them to put up several billion dollars to join with Paulson to insure these shaky mortgages. Paulson, to lure the "marks" into betting the billions, would pretend to put $200 million into the investment himself.

But, in fact, Paulson would be betting *against* those very mortgages. Paulson himself was the secret beneficiary of the "insurance" on the mortgages. When the housing market goes bust, Paulson would collect from the duped banks and they'd never even know it.

And Goldman would get a $15 million fee, or more, for lining up the sheep for the fleecing.

Goldman provided Paulson with a twenty-nine-year-old kid, a French neophyte, to play the shill, making presentations to the European buyers with a fancy, twenty-eight-page "flip-book" about the wonderful, secure set of home mortgages the "clients" would be buying.

The carefully selected bag of sick mortgages was packaged up into bundles totaling several billion dollars. To paint this turd gold, Paulson and Goldman brought in the well-respected risk-management firm of ACA Capital. Paulson personally met with ACA and gave them jive that he himself was investing in the insurance (as opposed to investing *against* the insurance).

The young punk that Goldman put on the case texted a friend (in French—*mais oui!*—about the inscrutable "*monstruosités*") while he was in the meeting with Paulson and ACA, right while Paulson was laying on the bullshit.

Secretly, Paulson personally designed the package of mortgages to load it up heavily with losers, concentrating on adjustable rate mortgages, like Pratt's, given to those with low credit scores, while culling out high-quality loans given by West Coast banker Wells Fargo. ACA, thinking Paulson was helping them pick the good stuff, put their valuable seal of approval on the mortgage packages, though they were quite nervous about their "reputation." (But that's what happens when you go out with bad boys.)

The mortgages in each package were dripping *dreck*— but with the ACA/Goldman stamp, Moody's and Standard & Poors gave the insurance policies a AAA rating. European banks that hold government pension invest- ments snapped up the AAA-rated junk.

Around August 7, 2008, the week I met with Pratt, his foreclosure and over a million others resulted in the Goldman mortgage securities losing 99 percent of their value. The Royal Bank of Scotland, left holding the bag, wrote a check to Goldman Sachs for just short of one billion ($840,909,090). Goldman did the honorable thing . . . and turned over the money to Paulson (after taking their slice).

Don't worry about the Royal Bank of Scotland. The British taxpayers and Bank of England covered its loss, taking over the bleeding bank.

And here's the brilliance of it: when it came out that Goldman and other mortgage-backed securities were simply hot steaming piles of manure, their value plummeted further and the mortgage market, already wounded, now collapsed—and mortgage defaults accel- erated nationwide. The result was that as the market plummeted, Paulson's profits skyrocketed: his hedge fund pulled in $3.5 billion and Paulson put over a billion of it in his own pocket.

With Paulson skinning some of Europe's leading banks for billions, there was a bit of a diplomatic and legal dustup. The SEC investigated, confirmed in detail Paulson's scam . . . and sued the kid at Goldman who acted as Paulson's assistant, the one who couldn't even follow the complex deal. Goldman paid a fine, admitted no wrongdoing.

And Paulson received . . . a tax break.

Pratt and several million others lost their homes, including a Saudi prince who, in the recession, had to sell his Vail, Colorado, home to Paulson for just $45 million.

■ ■ ■

But Detroit could not have died if its auto industry were not in a coma.

In 2008 and 2009, both Presidents Bush and Obama opened Treasury checkbooks to save the Great American Industry, with $80 billion in cash and loans for GM and Chrysler.

But the wheels were about to come off the bail-out.

Two men had quietly bought up GM's former auto-parts unit, Delphi Corporation, for sixteen cents a share. In 2009, when the bailout was ready to go, including a plan to save Delphi and its twenty-five thousand union jobs, the two hedge-fund speculators said, *Gotcha!* Unless they were paid ransom—about $12 billion—they would shut down crucial parts factories and bring every US auto assembly line to a deadly halt.

They had Obama, GM, and Chrysler by the ball bearings.

The two speculators, Singer the Vulture and John Paulson, got every dime they demanded. GM agreed to pay off $1.1 billion of Delphi's debts; forgave $2.15 billion owed Delphi by GM; pumped $1.75 billion into Delphi operations; and GM took over four money-losing parts plants, all the cash ultimately supplied from US taxpayer bailout funds.

Then there was the big one: the US Treasury would pay $6.2 billion in pensions owed to Delphi workers.

Paulson made $1.5 billion and Singer $900 million, thirty-two times their investment, when the stock went from sixteen cents to twenty-two *dollars* with the government cash.

The Vulture duo took the money—and ran. Only four out of forty-five Delphi parts plants remain in the US. Most of the rest shuttered, but some were moved to China. Every one of Delphi's twenty-one thousand UAW employees lost their job. All salaried workers at Delphi in Detroit had their pension money confiscated and eliminated.

And Robert Pratt lost his home and his vote.

Singer shared a piece of his big payday with the coinvestors of Elliott Management, the invitation-only fund that the Vulture used to take down Delphi.

Governor Mitt Romney was dead opposed to this "free pass" for Wall Street, standing with a square jaw against the Treasury forking over billions to bail out Detroit and the auto industry. "Let Detroit Go Bankrupt," the governor wrote in the *New York Times*.

Romney's position was principled—and surprising, given that the Romney family made its fortune in Detroit when Mitt's daddy became president of American Motors (now part of Chrysler).

Romney wrote, "Detroit needs a turnaround, not a check."

Then I looked at the auto scion's tax returns. Apparently, Mitt had dumped his interests in Chrysler. If Chrysler went down, well, that was the Pratt family's problem. Romney's trust had moved a few million to Elliott Management and got a slice of the 3,200 percent return from the bailout bonanza.

Romney took the check—and cashed it.

And he got another tax break, as did Singer and Paulson. It's called "carried interest." It allows the trio to pay a lesser tax rate on their $2.4 billion payoff than Pratt pays on his salary.

President Obama thinks that the "carried interest" tax loophole ought to be closed. And Paulson and Singer are not happy about that. They each ponied up a million dollars for Restore Our Future to pay for ads to attack Obama for letting America lose jobs.

■ ■ ■

So, what are you going to do about it?

Conclusion:
Mighty Stream

Jimmy Carter once said, "America should have a president as good as its people." Unfortunately, that's what we usually get. The Oval Office has been the residence of craven con-men, sanctimonious scoundrels, psychopathic blood worshippers, vainglorious vulgarities, rich dicks and wannabe rich dicks, fraudsters, fakers, and worse: hollow suits, scarecrows, chattering death masks, and men without meaning even to themselves.

Every four years Americans vote for the nightmare of their choice. And now, even that's being taken away. The billionaires' money-lubricated ballot bandit machinery, from purging to caging to nun-nullifying ID checks, is mauling the last sad shards of what was American democracy.

Is the solution campaign finance reform? Get real. No politician is going to vote to cut off their own juice.

You can't stop billionaires from spending their billions. The only way to put an end to billionaires buying our elections is to *put an end to billionaires*. Preferably nonviolently.

The Vulture, the Ice Man, Target 67C (Koch), Pat Robertson, Robert Rubin . . . all got their boodle from some kind of finance/petroleum/resource swindle. We're not talking about inventing the iPad here, or Oprah making a billion by helping us accept our own inadequacies. We're talking about characters who've made cruelty a profit center, who smash, grab, and lobby: staying one step ahead of prosecutors and regulators by buying—through political donations, payoffs, and lobbying power—changes to the law to legalize their cruelty and let them off the hook.

There's only one solution: *take away their billions*. When the Ice Man funds Karl Rove's attack on the right of a Hispanic to register to vote, that's just part of the process of Ice making his money off leaving lead paint in schools, then investing the sick profits in a toxic waste dump. The Ice Man's type of business requires a big legal team, public relations flacks, lobbyists, and a governor, a few congressmen, and a president or two.

When Singer the Vulture loads up super-PAC Restore Our Future, it's simply part of the protection money needed to protect the loot he's carrying out of the Congo. When King Leopold of Belgium raped the Congo, his colonial marauders used priests to bless their banditry. Today, the new *conquistadors* need politicians.

So what do we do? The fight to protect the right to vote, for civil rights, begins with the fight for economic rights: for the Pratt family in Detroit against Paulson's home foreclosure scam, for Ana Amparo's kid in New York fighting the Ice Man's lead poisons, for the Congolese fighting cholera and the Vulture, and for Stanlee Ann Mattingly and the Osage Indians to get their oil back from the Koch gang.

If you don't stop the Vultures from legally shoplifting the US auto industry and the Congo's cobalt, the predators will be so bloated with billions they will become too powerful to stop their legally burgling our elections.

Martin Luther King Jr. saw civil rights and economic justice as flowing together into the same "Mighty Stream."

> *"There must be a better distribution of wealth . . .*
> *for all God's children. Call it 'Democracy.'"*

This wee tome is not the place to tell you how to become an active advocate for economic justice, whether to Occupy, to march, to register, to tweet, to donate, to educate, and otherwise make yourself a pain in the ass to the 1 percent no-good-niks.

I will, however, give you a partial list of groups you might want to join up with and media sources that can inoculate you against the stupidity virus that infects US news reports.

Governor Granholm told me the key to voter protection is to "recognize your own power." And as the Reverend Jesse Jackson, who pushed me to write this book, said, "We've marched too long, we've worked too hard, and died too young" to let them steal our vote.

First, you have to *beat the ballot bandits.* Lock'm out of your ballot box.

Here are seven simple steps to take to protect yourself and your loved ones from ballot bandits. Take it out, reprint it, download copies at www.BallotBandits.org, and send it around, add it to your Facebook page, tattoo it around your nipple ring.

Then sign up with us for updates and new reports.

Dr. King gave us our marching orders:

> "*Human progress never rolls in on wheels of inevitability; it comes through the tireless efforts of men willing to be coworkers with God, and without this hard work, time itself becomes an ally of the forces of social stagnation. . . . Let us be dissatisfied until from every city hall, justice will roll down like waters and righteousness like a mighty stream.*"

Here's your paddle. . . .

7 Ways to Beat the Ballot Bandits

Join the Insurgency
Go to:
www.BallotBandits.org

TEAR ME OUT & SPREAD ME ABOUT!

1 Don't Go Postal!

For those of you who mailed in your ballot, please tell me, what happened to it? You don't know, do you? In the last election, half a million absentee ballots were never counted, on the flimsiest of technical excuses. And when they don't count, you don't even know it. Worse: Loads of ballots are not mailed out to voters in time to return them—in which case you're out of luck. Most states won't let you vote in-precinct once you've applied to vote absentee. Unless you absolutely have to mail in a ballot, don't go postal.

2 Vote Early—Before the Ballot Bandits Wake Up

You can vote before Election Day. Do it. Don't wait until Election Day to find out you have the wrong ID, your registration's "inactive" (9.9 million of you), or you're on some creep's challenge list. By Election Day, if your name is gone there's little you can do but hold up the line. And demand a *paper* ballot.

3 Register and Register, then Register Again

Think you're registered to vote? Think again, Jack. With all this purge'n going on (13 million and counting), you could be x'd out and you don't know it. So check online with your Secretary of State's office or County Board of Elections. Then register your girlfriend, your wife, your mailman, and your mommy. Then contact the Rainbow PUSH, LULAC, or Rock the Vote and volunteer to register folks, especially at social service agencies. In Florida, that means you'll get arrested. I'll send a file in a cake.

From ***Billionaires and Ballot Bandits:
How to Steal an Election in 9 Easy Steps***
by Greg Palast with Comic Book by Ted Rall

Vote Unconditionally, Not Provisionally

In November, they'll be handing out provisional ballots like candy, a couple million to Hispanic voters alone. If your right to vote is challenged, don't accept a provisional ballot that likely won't get counted no matter what the sweet little lady at the table tells you. She won't decide; partisan sharks will. Demand adjudication on the spot of your right to a real no-BS ballot from poll judges. Or demand a call to the supervisor of elections; or return with acceptable ID if that's the problem. And be a champ: defend the rights of others. If you've taken Step 1 above and voted early, you have Election Day free to be a poll watcher. Then challenge the challengers, the weird guys with Blackberrys containing lists of "suspect" voters. Be firm, but no biting.

Occupy Ohio, Invade Nevada

The revolution will not be podcast. Let go of that mouse, get out of your PJs, and take the resistance door-to-door—to register the vote, to canvass the voters, to get out the vote. Donate time to your union (if you're not in a union, why not?) or to the troublemakers listed here. This may seem a stupendously unoriginal suggestion, but it's still the best weapon for confronting the armed and dangerous junta that would seize the White House.

Date a Voter

Voting, like bowling and love, should never be done alone. As our sponsor, the Rev. Jesse Jackson says, make a date to "Arrive with Five." And keep a copy of *Billionaires & Ballot Bandits* in your holster; our website on your iStuff (we'll have help lines on our site), and a photo ID that matches your registration name and address. And Bobby, make sure your ID says, "Robert F. Kennedy JUNIOR"—or your vote is toast.

Make the Democracy Demand: No Vote Left Behind!

I have this crazy fantasy in my head. In it, an election is stolen and a million Americans stand up and say three magic words: "Count the votes." You can have all the paper ballots in the world, but if you don't demand to look at them, publicly, in a recount, you might as well mark them with invisible ink.

Democracy requires vigilance The Day After. That's when you check in at www.BallotBandits.org one more time.

Action Resources

Find out about the crucial work of these action groups—
and add your own—at *www.BallotBandits.org*.

Rainbow PUSH Coalition

Campus Election Engagement Project

Arizona Advocacy Network

League of United Latin American Citizens NM

Election Defense Alliance

Center for the Study of Democratic Societies

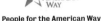
Rock the Vote

United Electrical, Radio and Machine Workers of America

Citizens for Election Integrity Minnesota

People for the American Way

Presente.org

CT Voters Count

Démos

Roots Action

Democracy North Carolina

Change to Win

Progress Now

Fair Elections Ohio

Public Citizen

Audit AZ

Justice Integrity Project

Head Count

Change.Org

MassVote

Immigrant Voting Project

Coalition to Expand Voting Rights

Move to Amend

One Arizona

Citizen Works

Oregon Peace Works

Peace and Justice Action League of Spokane

Long Distance Voter

Protect California Ballots

Protect our Elections Campaign

Protect the Count NH

Speak Out!

Stop Tarsands Oil Pipelines (Texas)

League of Humane Voters

Rio Grande Voter Registration Alliance (RGVRA)

Citizen Engagement Laboratory

Center for Hand–Counted Paper Ballots
Sheila Parks, Ed.D. | Sharona Merel

Big Apple Coffee Party

Unitarian Universalist Service Committee

Video the Vote

Voter March

Verified Voting – Wake County

Occupy Oakland

Code Pink

Global Exchange

SMALL PLANET INSTITUTE
Small Planet Institute
Frances Moore Lappé

National Action Network

USAction

Money Outta Politics
Rob Hager

Election Integrity

UNECO

Umatilla Morrow Alternatives

Want to add your own group? Go to *www.BallotBandits.org.*

Media Resources

Here are the no-BS outlets that cover our stories. Connect to them at
www.BallotBandits.org

Occupy.com

The Young Turks

The**Progressive**
SINCE 1909
The Progressive

Color of Change

N^{THE}ation.
The Nation

THOM HARTMANN
PROGRAM   News. Opinion. Debate.
Thom Hartmann Program
The Big Picture

the**guardian**
unitedstates
The Guardian US

Rolling Stone Magazine

Mother Jones
SMART, FEARLESS JOURNALISM
Mother Jones

Democracy Now!

firedoglake
Firedoglake

truthout
Truthout

EcoWatch
EcoWatch

BradBlog

**Media Matters
with Bob McChesney**

IN THESE TIMES
WITH LIBERTY AND JUSTICE FOR ALL.
In These Times

Nation of Change
Nation of Change

I.B.I.S. Radio
Radio with a View
WMBR – Radio with a View
Host: Dave Goodman

MARY BERG
Producer, A Musical Offering, KPFA

What Really Happened
Michael Rivero

The Political Grinder
The Political Grinder

PR Watch

AWAKENED AMERICA
Awakened America
Host: Marshall Stern

news from
UNDERGROUND
**Mark Crispin Miller's
News from Underground**

Antonia Juhasz
Antonia Juhasz

OCCUPIED
The Occupied Wall Street Journal

Project Censored

New Focus Radio Show
with Mike DeRosa

The Alex Bennet Show

KPFA – Morning Mix

Pros and Cons
of Controversial Issues

Progressive Voices

The Columbus Free Press
by Bob Fitrakis and Harvey Wasserman

This is Hell!
with Chuck Mertz

Daily Kos

On with Leon – XM 169
with Wilmer Leon, Ph.D.

Between the Lines

The Mudflats

The Shannyn Moore Show

WPKN 89.5 FM

Bree Walker

Carl Wolfson in the Morning
Producer: Paul Pimentel

Book Pleasures
Sandra Shwayder Sanchez

Buzzflash

Concentric Media
Dorothy Fadiman

Eco-Logic

John Perkins

KAOS

KBOO – Voices from the Edge
Host: Dave Mazza

Left Jab Radio

New Paradigm Digest

OB Rag

Rob Kall

Roland Sheppard's
Web Page
Roland Sheppard

RONNIE DUGGER
THE FREE MAN
Ronnie Dugger

Roseanne Barr

Reader
The San Diego Reader
Dave Rice | Journalist

The SoonerThought Show

Surreal News

Free Forum
Terrence McNally

Mike Feder

The Meria Heller Show

News Dissector
Danny Schechter

The Solution Zone
Host: Christiane Brown

Velvet Revolution

The West Coast Truth

WWRL – The Morning Show
Host: Mark Riley

Lizz Winstead

Tikkun

Suicide Girls
Nicole Powers

WORT fm
Host: Norman Stockwell

OpEd News

Free Speech TV

Razorcake
Chris Pepus

Link TV

Progressive News Network

The Nicole Sandler Show

Alternative Tentacles
Jello Biafra

The Real News Network

KPFA–Flashpoints
with Dennis Bernstein

Ring of Fire Radio

Gary Null

KPFT – The Monitor

Grit TV
Host: Laura Flanders

Indymedia

Harper's Magazine

Hightower Lowdown

Consortium News | Robert Parry

Alternet

The Stephanie Miller Show

The Indypendent

Cold Type

Dollars & Sense Magazine

Free Speech Radio News

The Konformist

Living Justice Press

The Pat Thurston Show – KGO

Morphizm
Scott Thill

The War Room
with Jennifer Granholm

YES! Magazine

Z Net

Fighting Bob

Lee Camp

Qualified Laughter

Alaska Commons
John and Heather Aronno

SIRIUSXM
LEFT
Make It Plain
Host: Mark Thompson

KKFI Community Radio
Tell Somebody
KKFI – Tell Somebody
Host: Tom Klammer

the karel show
The Karel Show
Host: Charles Karel Bouley

KGNU

KUNM

WRFG – Radio Free Georgia

John Wellington Ennis

SAM LAND
Sam Mayfield

WPFW
Raucous Caucus
Raucous Caucus – WPFW
Hosts: Terry D. Kester | Mark Levine |
Garland Nixon

MAKING CONTACT
Women Rising Radio Project

Brainfood from the Heartland
The Louie b. Free Radio Show
The Louie B. Free Show

WPFW
WHAT'S AT STAKE
What's at Stake – WPFW
Hosts: Verna Avery Brown | Terry D. Kester

bullfrogfilms
Bullfrog Films

KPFA 94.1 fm

WPFW
Pacifica Radio Washington, D.C.

WVOX - Environmentally Sound
Host: Bob Lebensold

The Matthew Filipowicz Show

KPFT 90.1 fm

Voices with Vision – WPFW
Hosts: Netfa Freeman | Naji Mujahid | Ryme Katkhouda

Sounds of Dissent
WZBC – Sounds of Dissent
Host: John Grebe

Scott Horton's Radio Shows

WBAI 99.5 fm

Marta Steele

The Mike Malloy Show

The Rick Smith Show

Pirate Television

KEXP–Mind over Matters
Host: Mike McCormick

Tom Dispatch

Sexy Liberal Comedy

SPECIAL THANKS TO

Ed Asner
Stanley & Betty Sheinbaum
Graham Nash
David Crosby
Jackson Browne
Neil Young
Willie Nelson
Boots Riley
Martin Sheen
Kelly Slater
Norman Lear
Chris Shiflett
Bree Walker
Bill Perkins
Roseanne Barr
Mike Pappantonio
Benno Friedman
Anne Meara & Jerry Stiller

funding provided by
PUFFIN FOUNDATION

CLOUD MOUNTAIN FOUNDATION

The Nation Institute
DEDICATED TO A FREE & INDEPENDENT PRESS

DONORS TO THE PALAST INVESTIGATIVE FUND

A 501C3 CHARITABLE TRUST PROJECT

Executive Producers

Benno Friedman
Donna Mae Litowitz
Mike & Sheila Wilkins
Bill Perkins
Joey Kaempfer
Danila Oder
Steve Kelem
Timothy Finn
Helen Shoup
Frank & Renee Kovacs
Dale Polekoff
Anne Brown
Rory Lewis
Richard Simpson
Andrew Tobias
Robert & Chandra Friese
Barbara Kramer
Patricia Morrison
Allen Michaan
James Yedor
Judd Williams
Harvey Glasser
Cary Franklin
Amy Shrack
John Ryan
Shirley Ross Davies

David Riley
Elena Anzalone
Dan Beach
Michael Caplice
Stephen Church
Todd Diehl
James & Dorothy Fadiman
Diane L. Fahey
Michael Finn
Joel Gaalswyk, *in memorium*
Brandon Gant
Rose Gapinski
John Gilpin
Joy Glatz
Brian Joiner
M L McGaughran
Cindy Moeckel
Stuart Pollock
Janette Rainwater
Alex Sadowsky
Doris Selz
George "Tony" Shanahan
Erik Sjoberg
Dianne Thiel
Lana Tolman
William Veale
Fay Cullen Inc

Associate Producers

Ian Graham
Susan Haugerud
Michael Kieschnick
Blair Koch

Anne Posel
Karl Wills
David Thomas
Maggie Dostal

Janis Weisbrot
Gladys Palast

Supporters

Dolores Boot
Virginia Laddey
Paul Gottlieb
Karl Wills
Jerry Boyles
William Hoffman
Todd Arena
Gavin Greer
JoAnn O'Linger-Luscusk
Donald Schreiber
Win Phelps
Winnie Foster
David Camarda
Stephen Garcia
Richard Wayne
Rainer Schwarz
Rudolph Rasin
Frank Knowles
Gerhard Bedding
Steve Snelling
Edith Conrad
Kyla Boyse
David Allegoren
Arthur Kennedy
Gail Coffey
Sally McCoy
Clarence Goldberg
Stephen Fischer
Susan Sheinfeld
Mark Passell
Eugene Desavouret
Mary Jurmain
Roger Diggle
Simone DeLeeuw
Francis Henry
Jose Bonetti
Tim Kirk
David Hale

Lucius Sorrentino
Susan Kidder
GreyBeard Design Group
Dewey O'Kelley
Elaine Phelps
Andre Parrish
Lana Touchstone
Elaine Taylor
Henry Hain
Gary James
Gary Kah
Joseph Holder
David Bellak
Ann Brennan
John Skinger
Anthony Sabo
Karen Boerboom
Laurie Kunkel
Hilarita Hogan
Mariah Lovejoy
Debbie Hodgson
Alan Meerow
Thomas McGaffey
Robert Chatel
Curtis Draves
David Merrick
Hedwin Naimark
Truit Trowbridge
Steve Turner
John Lavelle
Carrie Biggs-Adams
Rick Doty
Val Zampedro
Barbara Tegge
Heather Thomas
Michael Bailey
Robert Trimper
James Manley

John Smith
Robert Goodrich
William Lamme
Bonnie Hong
Charles Freas
David Huffman
George Williams
Colin Glover
Anthony Spanovic
Megan McCarthy
William Arnold
Jane Allen
Shirley Basso
Patricia Bauerle
Ken Brown
Russell Burlingame
Henry Chen
Steve Coatney
Deborah Copeland Bruno
Christine Csernica-Haas
Anna Donners
Henrik Dusek
Nils Essle
Robert Friend
Kathryn Goodman
Barbara Gummere
Henry Hain III
Martin Hendel
Sally Herklots
Laurie Hester
Elaine Hyatt
Robert James
Wendelin Johnson
Liz Kaiser
Eugenia Kalnay
Mary Kathleen Reuter
Joyce Kidd
Stanley Kopacz

Zachary Kramer
Carsten Kuckuk
Lorie Lindsey
James Lint
Christopher Lish
Mariah Lovejoy
Thomas McGaffey
Alan Meerow
Jim Miller
Josie Mirek
Gavin Mitchell
Kris Nielsen
Andre Parrish
Mark Passell
Peter Payne
Michael Pearce
Perry Pearson
Mary Reuter
Vernon Rholl
Richard Rosenthal
Gail Ross
Donald Schreiber
Mike Selig
Bobby Shew
Charles Varni
Alison Williams
George Wolf
Eleanor Wood Bell
Elizabeth Fraser
Dale Robinson
Frank Knowles
Linnea Austad
Lorena Monda
Barry Benjamin
Leroy Pletten
Michael Walsh
Lawrence Smith Jr.
Benjamin Visuals

NOTES ON CALCULATIONS

Don't be deceived by the fact that this book takes a populist approach and includes a comic book. *Billionaires & Ballot Bandits* remains a rigorous treatise on the source of financial flows influencing US elections with an analytical investigation of the substantial ballot loss rates and growing registration impediments in the US. Of necessity, the work behind this investigation includes summarizing complex data and statistics.

All calculations are derived from data supplied by the US Elections Assistance Commission based on 133,944,538 voters participating in the 2008 election as reported by 4,517 jurisdictions (USEAC *2008 Election Administration and Voting Survey*). Calculations adjust for EAC inclusion of nonintegral territorial voters (Puerto Rico, American Samoa, Virgin Islands), and incomplete survey reports from jurisdictions. Absentee count rates combine with the separate reporting by the EAC of UOCAVA (Uniformed and Overseas Citizens Absentee Voting Act) participants.

Spoilage rates determined from undervote and overvote are derived from: Election Data Services Inc., 2004 Election Day Survey Report, Part 2 Survey Results, Overvotes and Undervotes (for USEAC) applied to 2008 data. Registration removals and rejections taken from USEAC Election and Administration and Voting Survey Tables, applications processed, list maintenance, and removal notices.

Note: the EAC states that "significant gaps remain in election data collection," and that shortcoming carries into our own data sets though best efforts are made to account for missing data. Thus the phrase, "No fewer than . . ." in stating the undercount and registration removals.

Thanks to Professors Matthew Barreto of the University of Washington and Philip Klinkner of Hamilton College, Dr. Tova Wang (formerly of the EAC), the staff of the the Brennan Center for Justice at New York University Law School, Dean Christopher Edley of the University of California Law School (former EAC Commissioner and cofounder of the Harvard University Law School Civil Rights Project) for their analyses of the racial profile of uncounted ballots and voters and for guidance in these calculations, though final responsibility rests fully on the author. The author's own skills, a bit rusty from his days teaching statistics at the University of Indiana, could not have been up to the task without the guidance of the work of these eminent and thoughtful scholars.

Further discussion and updates of the calculations appear as they become available at www.BallotBandits.org, as well as the commentaries and findings of the experts listed above. Credentialed experts are invited to post their own findings for group analysis.

—Greg Palast

INDEX

ALSO BY TED RALL

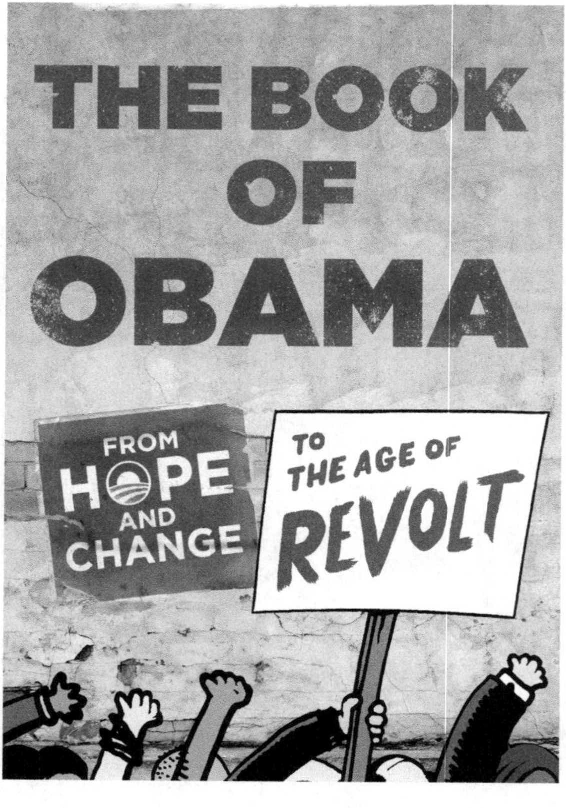
THE BOOK OF OBAMA
FROM HOPE AND CHANGE
TO THE AGE OF REVOLT

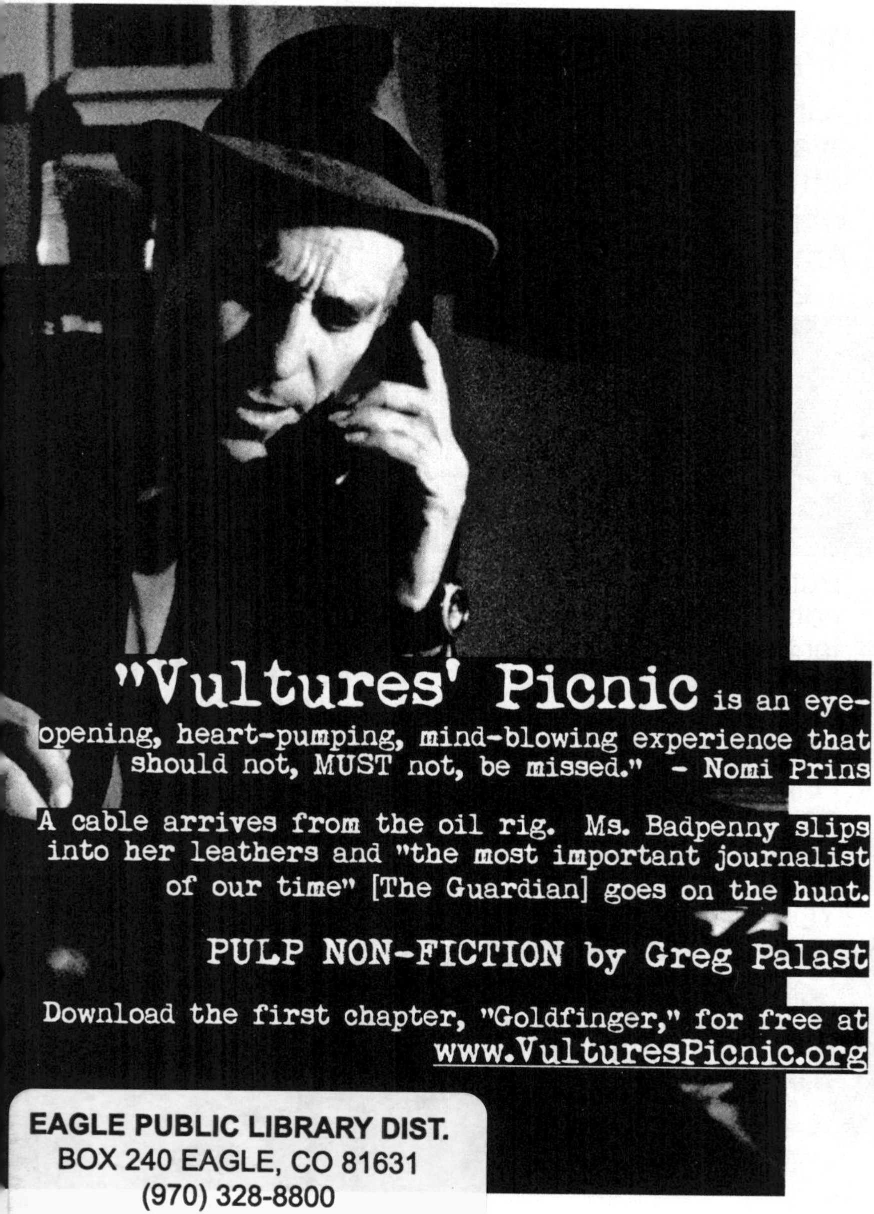
"Vultures' Picnic is an eye-opening, heart-pumping, mind-blowing experience that should not, MUST not, be missed." - Nomi Prins
A cable arrives from the oil rig. Ms. Badpenny slips into her leathers and "the most important journalist of our time" [The Guardian] goes on the hunt.
PULP NON-FICTION by Greg Palast
Download the first chapter, "Goldfinger," for free at www.VulturesPicnic.org

PALASTINVESTIGATIVEFUND